THE LOVE PLAN
NOW YOU CAN MAKE IT HAPPEN—
AND MAKE IT LAST!

Have you ever wondered what *she* had that you didn't? Now the secret's out. The answers are all here. Whether you're sixteen or sixty, single or married, Tracy Cabot shows you how to—

- BREAK OUT OF "THE BASTARD TRAP"
- RECOGNIZE THE MAN WHO'S RIGHT FOR YOU
- ASSURE RETURN ENGAGEMENTS
- SETTLE ACCOUNTS WITHOUT CONFLICT
- LEARN WHAT MAKES A MAN FALL TOTALLY IN LOVE—with you
- KNOW HOW MUCH TO GIVE—and how soon
- IGNITE A LIFETIME LOVE AFFAIR

Tracy Cabot has been using these techniques to help other women develop successful love relationships. She's used them herself, as well, to find that at age forty-two, she was a bride herself for the very first time! Scientifically proven, The Love Plan is guaranteed to work—for you!

Also by Tracy Cabot

Letting Go (with Dr. Zev Wanderer)
How to Keep a Man in Love with You Forever

QUANTITY SALES

Most Dell books are available at special quantity discounts when purchased in bulk by corporations, organizations, or groups. Special imprints, messages, and excerpts can be produced to meet your needs. For more information, write to: Dell Publishing, 1540 Broadway, New York, NY 10036. Attention: Special Markets.

INDIVIDUAL SALES

Are there any Dell books you want but cannot find in your local stores? If so, you can order them directly from us. You can get any Dell book currently in print. For a complete up-to-date listing of our books and information on how to order, write to: Dell Readers Service, Box DR, 1540 Broadway, New York, NY 10036.

How to Make a Man Fall in Love With You

TRACY CABOT

A DELL BOOK

Published by
Dell Publishing
a division of
Random House, Inc.

To my husband, Marshall

If you purchased this book without a cover you should be aware that this book is stolen property. It was reported as "unsold and destroyed" to the publisher and neither the author nor the publisher has received any payment for this "stripped book."

Copyright © 1984 by Tracy Cabot

All rights reserved. No part of this book may be reproduced or transmitted in any form or by any means, electronic or mechanical, including photocopying, recording, or by any information storage and retrieval system, without the written permission of the Publisher, except where permitted by law. For information address: St. Martin's Press, Inc., New York, New York.

The trademark Dell® is registered in the U.S. Patent and Trademark Office.

ISBN: 0-440-14536-8

Reprinted by arrangement with St. Martin's Press, Inc.

Printed in the United States of America

One Previous Dell Trade Paperback Edition

February 1987

OPM 29 28 27 26 25 24 23 22

Acknowledgments

Without the faith of my trusting friends who first put their love lives in my hands, this book would never have been written. Also, grateful thanks to those others whose ideas and energy helped in so many ways: Robert Leighton, Bernadette McNulty, Allen Harris, my editor, Toni Lopopolo, my agent, Tom Goff, Betsy Berkhemer, Ben Blank, Ruth Blank, Ruth Halcomb, Terri Mayo, Judy Rosen and Nancy Shiffrin.

Contents

Acknowledgments 5
A Personal Note from the Author 12
Introduction 15
Preface 17

1. CRAZY LOVE 23

What Not to Do 26
Crazy Love 31

2. BREAKING OUT OF "THE BASTARD TRAP" 34

First Signs 35
Bastards Are Sexy 36
Ten Classic Bastard Types 37
The Achiever • The Guru • The Timebomb • The Waffler • The Supervisor • The Carpetbagger • The Dealer • The Patient • The Cripple • The Fairy Godfather
First Aid for Bastard Sufferers 50
Bastard Checklist 50
Bastard Survival Strategy 52

3. YOUR PERSONAL "MAN PLAN" 54

Your Requirements 56
Visualizing 57
Sample Man Plan 60
Qualifiers 65

4. YOUR SEARCH PLAN 68

The Commitment 69
The Value of "Volume" 70
Open Searching 71
Your "Volume" Approach 72
Your Primary Search Activity 72
Specific Ways of Meeting Men 74
What Do You Say? 79

5. WHY MEN LOVE: A NEW WAY TO GET CLOSE 82

The Chemistry of Love 85
The First Date 86
Missed Connections 88
Discovering His Love Language 90

6. THE VISUAL MAN 95

Reading His Eyes 96
The Visual Personality 99
Visual Expressions 102
How to Make Love to the Visual Man 104
What You Are 106

7. THE AUDITORY MAN 108

Auditory Eyes 108
The Auditory Personality 113

How to Make Love to the Auditory Man 118
What You Are 120

8. THE FEELINGS MAN 121

Feeling Eyes 121
The Feelings Personality 125
How to Make Love to the Feelings Man 128
What You Are 129

9. SECRET REFLECTIONS 131

Being "In Tune" 132
Physical Mirroring 133
What Shall I Wear? 138

10. MORE SECRET REFLECTIONS 142

Mirroring Rhythms 142
Mirroring Breathing 143
Mirroring Life Rhythms 144
Mirroring Volume 146
Mirroring Belief Systems 149

11. ANCHORING YOUR LOVE 153

Anchoring Happy Feelings 153
Anchoring Sexy Feelings 156
Anchoring to Solve Problems 159

12. GETTING HIM TO DO WHAT YOU WANT IN BED 163

Pillowtalk that Works 165
Sexual Teasing 167
Show and Tell 169

Getting Him in the Mood 170
"Method Sex" 171

13. HOW MUCH TO GIVE AND HOW SOON 175

Giving Too Much Too Soon 176
Neediness Turns Men Off 178
The Danger of Overromanticizing Too Soon 179
Time Wasters 180
How Much to Tell 181
When Overgiving Starts 183
When to Give Your All 190

14. ASSURING RETURN ENGAGEMENTS 191

Subtle Triggers 193
Building an Instant History 194
The Podium Effect 196
Repetition 197
Our Song 199
Praise 199

15. HANDLING LOVE'S PROBLEMS 201

Controlling Fear of Loss 202
Mirroring His Ideas 204
What He Doesn't Say 206
Other Women 207
Your Jealousy 208
His Jealousy 211
Preventing Jealousy 212
Why We Get Jealous 213

16. DON'T FIGHT 215

Reflecting 217
Venting 218
Self-Disclosure 220
Winning with Humor 221
"Broken Record" 222
Agreement 225
Negotiating 226

17. CASTING A SPELL 229

Don't Use It Unless You're Sure 231
That Old Black Magic 232
Weaving It All Together 243

18. WHEN LOVE HAPPENS 245

Clinching the Commitment 247
Who Asks? 248
Overcoming Resistance 251
Advice from Friends 253
Don't Screw It Up 254
Keeping Love Alive 255

A Personal Note from the Author

I was over thirty-five and still answering those embarrassing questions like, "How come you've never been married?" and "Do you live all alone in this big house?" or, "Don't you have a boyfriend that you're serious about?"

In an otherwise successful life, I had failed in "Meaningful Relationship I" and probably would have continued to do so if I hadn't discovered the scientific secrets for loving that make up The Love Plan.

Until then, my life was one relationship after another. I fell in love over and over again, but each time the affair ended in a disastrous breakup.

Although I had lots of opportunities with all kinds of men (some terrific, some not too great), I was never able to make love work out right before I began using The Love Plan. My relationships were so terrible, I became an expert at breaking up and even wrote a book on the subject *(Letting Go,* Warner, 1979), using all my failures as examples.

Letting Go helped a lot of people get over their broken hearts and I was always gratified to meet someone who had read the book and felt better. But the more I talked to people about getting over the loss of a love, the more it became clear that what they really wanted was not to lose that love in the first place. Down deep, what they really wanted was a good love relationship, to love and be loved back.

"Why not?" they wanted to know. "Love is so right, so basic! Why is it so damn hard to find?"

Right then, I decided to spend as much time as it might take to discover what really makes love work. I spent nearly two full years researching the subject of love—and found no answers. Then, unexpectedly, while reading an obscure article about the psychology of human communications, everything "clicked" into place.

These new psychological findings, I realized with a rush of excitement, were the long-missing link in the mystery of love. There, before my eyes, was the explanation for why a few women seemed to find true love effortlessly—while the rest of us don't.

These new discoveries about human behavior meshed totally with my other research and my own experiences. They filled in every gap in the Love Problem.

Putting it all together, I realized that I had even more than the explanations I wanted about why true love is so elusive. What it all added up to was a coherent, precise blueprint for finding love. At that moment, I knew I had discovered The Love Plan.

At first, it seemed too good to be true. So quietly, tentatively, I began to experiment with myself and a few trusted friends. Our sudden success in finding love was so apparent that others became curious. Soon my phone was ringing day and night with calls from people wanting to know the mysterious secret.

In the beginning, I just made suggestions. Then I started handing out xeroxed notes.

Somewhat awestruck, I watched The Love Plan create the "chemistry" of love, again and again. I grew more adept at explaining The Love Plan—and finally became determined to write this book.

The techniques in *How to Make a Man Fall in Love with You* work. I know because they have worked for me and everyone else who has tried them—even women who thought love had passed them by. Because I had these insights and had learned these techniques, I was ready for a real relationship when I met the right man. I knew what to do.

In the past, I would have ruined my chances with this relationship in the same way I had with the disasters that preceded it. Instead, I used The Love Plan approach.

Now, for the first time (in my forties), I am married and building a life together with someone I love.

I hope that by faithfully following The Love Plan, everyone who reads *How to Make a Man Fall in Love with You* will be as happy as I am.

—T.C.

Introduction

Hardly anyone can resist an offer of more love. Getting love is the inspiration for the greatest works of art, for the most brilliant performances, for the world's memorable poems and great literature. Behind our striving for success and recognition, for good looks, knowledge, intimacy and communication is a simple desire to be loved.

In a world of searching and insecurity, of singles' bars and midlife crises, dating services and therapy groups, there is a desperate shortage of mature, mutual love. Millions of women, ready for a loving, committed relationship, are unable to find it. These women can now be helped.

How to Make a Man Fall in Love with You is for every woman who isn't getting all the love she wants right now.

Preface

People who are in love communicate on a level that surpasses the mundane and reaches deep into the other person's psyche. Lovers seem to read each other's minds, to know ahead of time what the other one is thinking.

They have made contact with each other's inner being. That's what the "chemistry" is, and that's what *you* are about to learn to create—at *your* will, with the man of *your* choice.

If you faithfully follow The Love Plan, you will never again have that desperate, helpless feeling of passively waiting for the "chemistry" of true love to randomly enter your life.

In order to make a man fall in love with you, you must first understand how he perceives his world. Then you can find the key to his heart. The Love Plan will show you the way.

How many times have you thought, "Oh, if only he knew how I felt! If only I could get through to him. Why can't he appreciate me? Can't he see how much I love him, how much I have to offer?" Now, by learning and using the insights and techniques embodied in The Love Plan, you can win the man of your dreams forever.

As you know, three of the basic human senses are: sight, sound, and feelings. New findings in psychology tell us that, for each person, one of these senses tends to dominate. A man tends to be either sight, sound, or feelings oriented. This is how he perceives his universe. It is the basis of his personality, his inner "Love Language," and, if understood properly, the key to his heart.

The Love Plan will show you how to find out your man's secret Love Language. You will discover whether he's a "seeing," "hearing," or "feeling" type. You will learn to talk to him in the special words he'll immediately relate to. You will act in ways that rivet his attention on you. You will make him feel as if you are his soul mate. You alone will truly understand him. Even the most elusive lover will be irresistibly under your spell.

You will sense his inner pleasures and pains. Like the great lovers of history, you'll know the perfect words to say. You'll have the faultless timing, the undeniable allure of really understanding him and his universe. Then you can make his heart belong to you forever.

A very few people—often the most successful people—use these techniques unconsciously, automatically. Great trial lawyers use them to appeal to judges and juries. Million-dollar salesmen use them to appeal to clients. Famous therapists use them to help people. Now, for the first time, you can learn how to use these scientific psychological discoveries to bring True Love into your life.

When I first suggested this powerful Love Plan to make a man fall in love with you, a few women (and men too) felt it wouldn't be fair. They felt that "making" someone fall in love with you would be manipulative, unromantic and cold. They felt it would be bypassing the "chemistry" and "magic" that love is supposed to be.

Yet these same women spend fortunes to color their hair and dress provocatively. They never go out without full makeup and a blow dry to make "less" look like "more." You probably know many women who diet to starvation—even have plastic surgery to turn up their noses and unlid their eyes—all in hopes of finding lasting love.

These are the women who truly believe that physical subterfuge is an acceptable part of the "all's fair in love" philosophy, while condemning strategies for better communication as dishonest. Of course, these are the same women who complain that men are unfeeling and don't understand them.

Our culture (and our economy) programs us to believe that beauty and youth are the prime trading commodities for love. But beauty and youth have never guaranteed love. In fact, true love is just as often found by those who are not young and beautiful. Everyone needs love. That's why The Love Plan is based on something everyone possesses—an inner ability to communicate.

Even though romantic love is supposed to be nonmanipulative, free of game playing, nondevisive, and free flowing, we find many methods of pressuring and convincing those we love to love us back. From Helen Gurley Brown's "Teddy Bear Tricks" in *Sex and the Single Girl,* to Marabel Morgan's *Joy of Womanhood,* Xavier Hollander's *Happy Hooker,* Alex Comfort's *Joy of Sex* and *More Joy,* and in classics like *Sex Without Guilt*—even in Dr. Reuben's *Everything You Always Wanted to Know About Sex* —we have learned some superficial ways to get more love.

Perhaps, says one, it's okay to lie, sneak, and cheat just a little. Another says to dress up. Some others recommend exotic sex acts, and the classics tell us we shouldn't feel guilty in bed. These days, any woman who's so inclined can learn to perform sexually just by reading the popular magazines. Even *Reader's Digest* tells us how to be good in bed.

Unfortunately, being good in bed is no guarantee of love, either. Even the most accomplished lover, surrounded by men, can find herself alone and yearning for a long-term, committed relationship. It's time to discover the real ways to make someone fall in love with you, not the superficial ones.

Until now, the deeper psychological techniques of unconscious motivation described in The Love Plan have been the private and protected secrets of a select group of researchers, divulged only to an exclusive few who could afford to attend expensive weeklong seminars costing thousands of dollars.

These strategic communication abilities are far more powerful than the teddy bear tricks you tried in the past, more enticing than any seduction, more lasting and effective than the greatest sexual performance. It seems only fair that they be available to everyone. What better use could they find than to bring more love into people's lives?

Combining these new communication strategies with well-known psychological techniques like "mirroring" and "anchoring," any woman can make a man fall in love with her.

The Love Plan shows how. But first, The Love Plan shows you how to pick the right man and avoid all the wrong ones.

Crazy Love

1

HIS PRESENCE LIT UP THE ROOM. THEN, WITH THE kind of animal magnetism that drives women crazy, he smiled at me and suddenly some primal bell went off.

I was driven to possess him, to make him mine with sexual pleasures he'd never imagined. Surely, if he knew the real me, if I gave him my all, he would be mine.

I loved him more than anything. I somehow felt secure when he was around, which was never enough. He was my life. I knew we were destined to be together. He was *supposed* to be mine.

I spent countless hours scheming and daydreaming about making him mine. If he called, I dropped everything and ran. Then one day he found someone else.

I thought my life would never be the same again. I needed to feel his body next to mine. I went to sleep thinking about him and woke up thinking about him.

In my dreams he was making wonderful love to me. Gently he would undress me, adoring each part of me, willing to postpone his pleasure for a few painfully beautiful instants more in order to admire me, his one and only love.

Waking alone, I was desperate. I would do anything to get him back again. Worse yet, I was just one of many women who felt that way about him. So what did I do?

When I look back and remember the awful, embarrassing things I did to make him love me, it makes me sad because it was all so useless.

I did *everything,* starting with the obvious—trying to make myself the most beautiful creature he'd ever seen. I devoured the beauty makeover books. I lost weight and exercised. I became more attractive, but still he wasn't mine.

Next I tried the sex route. I gorged myself with *The Joy of Sex,* and then *More Joy,* and *Even More Joy.* I studied Xavier Hollander and Dr. Reuben. I became an expert on what part of his body to touch when and where, on pleasuring his masculinity in ways he'd never been pleasured before.

It wasn't long before he was tempted by my increasing sexuality and wilder and wilder exploits. He was back in my bed, but deep down, I knew he didn't really love me.

Undaunted, I decided to make him dependent on

me. I alone would fulfill his every desire. If he was missing a sock, I'd be the one to find it for him. If he had to catch a plane, I would take him to the airport. If he needed to meet someone important for his business, I would arrange the connection. If he wanted to make love, I was always there.

I provided everything he wanted—yet he didn't love me. Deep inside I knew it and I began to scheme, becoming more and more frantic in my attempts to get the man I loved to love me back. I was willing to try anything. . . .

As a journalist, I was often invited to places he wasn't—for example, Sandstone, the notorious free love community in southern California made famous in Gay Talese's book, *Thy Neighbor's Wife.* Giving "The Sandstone Experience" to this man I wanted so badly was one more last-ditch attempt to bond him to me. Naturally it backfired.

Since part of The Sandstone Experience was making love to whomever you wanted whenever you wanted, the man I adored was soon enjoying "The Experience" on his own with other ladies and I was left once again. Of course, eventually, so were they.

Then, like a summer storm, he blew back into my life. Had I learned my lesson? Did I tell him to get lost? No, I was to take him back over and over again, repeating the get-nowhere pattern with him—and with other men after him. Meanwhile, I realized there must be something I was doing wrong or some secret I didn't know.

I studied intricate love games and listened to old wives' tales. I interviewed happily married women, kept women, expensive call girls and madams across the United States to find out their secrets. I talked to women who got love easily. I met with psychologists and read every book on the subject of love and sex. But I was unable to get the love I knew I deserved, no matter what—until I discovered The Love Plan.

The secrets of getting a man to fall in love with you have been hidden for too long. Any woman who is halfway attractive can probably find someone to go to bed with her. But that's not what most women want. Or most men either. According to the latest *Playboy* polls, men rank sex as fourth after love and family and relationships. Men and women both want something more than sex.

As women we want that ultimate commitment when a man says, "I love you and never want to leave you." The real love that lasts for a lifetime is what we want. That love is possible if you know how to reach the soul of the man you want. The Love Plan will teach you how.

You deserve all the love you are capable of returning. If you don't have it right this minute, you are being cheated of one of life's greatest joys.

If you will follow The Love Plan steps without deviating—without falling back on the dumb things we've all tried in the past—I guarantee you won't fail.

What Not to Do

Just in case you aren't sure which things you're *not* supposed to do, I'm going to give you some real-life examples. You may recognize a few you've tried, or you may be grateful you've never been that desperate.

Suicide

"I tried suicide twice," an attractive twenty-seven-year old advertising executive told me. "'I can't live without you,' I told him, and took a whole bottle of aspirin. I slept for a day, and when I woke up he wasn't there. Of course, I never meant to kill myself, just to make him feel too guilty to leave me."

Lots of women try suicide to get a man's attention. It sometimes works. Some women succeed in dying and some even get their man, but just for a short time.

No man in his right mind is going to make a long-term commitment to a suicidal woman. Suicide attempts usually only get his pity until he feels safe getting out. The same goes for pregnancy, real or pretend, especially in today's world of easy termination.

Pregnancy

"I lied and said I was pregnant," a sexy and otherwise intelligent medical secretary in her early thirties told me. "It turned out to be terrible because all he wanted to do was make sure I got an abortion as quickly as possible. He offered me money, but he didn't offer to marry me—or even to go with me for the abortion (which was just as well since I wasn't pregnant).

"One lie led to another. Because I had pretended to be pregnant, I then had to pretend I had the abortion, so I shaved my pubic hairs. Once I even injected myself with sterile water in front of him in a fake abortion attempt, but he was unmoved. I wanted to show him I had made the supreme sacrifice, and he didn't even care."

BRIBES

A thirty-three-year-old beauty shop owner told me, "I gave him money. Thousands and thousands of dollars, maybe ten thousand over the years. I figured there would be an economical bonding since I knew he wanted to be rich. He said he was investing it for 'our' future. He took my money, but he didn't do what I wanted, which was to love me enough to marry me. He met another woman and now we're in court over the real estate he bought with my money. 'I loved the money, not you' is what he said when he left."

Bribery is a tactic many women have tried on a man. It's cheap and embarrassing. Even when it works, bribery makes you lose respect for the man because he's so weak. One of the most desperate women I talked to admitted to me that she had tried to bribe a man she was trying to captivate with drugs.

"I had to admit to myself what I was doing after a while," this successful television actress confided to me. "I was spending almost two thousand dollars a month on cocaine. I tried to get him hooked on the drug. Then I figured I could always have him when I wanted him by offering more.

"I bought him a little silver coke spoon and a mirror that said 'You're wonderful' on it. Whenever he walked in my door, there were little white lines on the coffee table to greet him. He fell in love with someone else anyway.

"During our relationship I spent over seven thousand dollars in six months on keeping us both stoned. All I wound up with was a habit and a broken heart."

Women have told me about bribing men with everything from trips, fancy cars and expensive clothes, to hard-to-get concert and theatre tickets, even houses and boats. Sure, it all works for maybe one date or two, or even a few months while he's accepting your goodies. But in between collecting whatever you have to offer and paying you back with a few precious moments of his time, you can never be sure he isn't out there falling in love with someone else. You simply can't buy love, no matter how rich you are.

Jealousy

And who hasn't tried making him jealous? From silly tricks like sending yourself a bouquet before he comes over or having a girl friend call while he's there and pretend to be some other man, to more elaborate plans, jealousy is dangerous and often backfires. One woman told me how she tried to use jealousy to capture a man's love, and lost him instead.

"I found out he had another woman he was seeing. I went crazy with jealousy. I wanted to kill her. I wanted my man back. I couldn't think of anything except them making love together. It was driving me crazy.

"I decided to make him jealous too, so I had an affair with the best-looking guy I could find, and I didn't make any secret of it. Then he thought he could hop into bed with anybody, if I did.

" 'Sure,' I lied to him, 'It doesn't matter to me.

Sleep with whoever you want.' We even went to a swing club together and he made love to another woman right in front of me.

"I thought my heart would break, but I was too proud to let him know it, so I made love to someone right in front of him. Soon, he made love to two more women. I made love to some more men. We kept trying to outdo each other.

"Then one day he told me he had fallen in love with another woman. She wouldn't play around and neither would he. I couldn't believe it. They were going to be faithful to each other."

Women have reported becoming swingers, exhibitionists, even bisexuals, to capture the fancy of some capricious male. He almost always gets away.

Infiltration

Infiltration is another entrapment technique that doesn't work. A twenty-five-year-old public relations assistant had mapped out a detailed infiltration plan for the man she wanted just as if she were trying to get close to a big new PR client. "I planned to make myself indispensable to him, to make him think he couldn't live without me.

"I made friends with his whole family and never missed an opportunity to send a card for a birthday or any other holiday. Christmas, New Year's, Valentine's Day, I never missed one. I even invited his mother to come and stay with me when she was visiting.

"I took photographs at family events and afterward I made up little albums of pictures and sent them to all his relatives. I took his nephews to Disneyland. I was showing him what a perfect wife I'd be. I even did his laundry.

"What a horrible surprise I got when he married a woman who didn't do anything for him. I never was able to figure out what he saw in her."

Crazy Love

All these women are involved in healthy relationships now, but they had to unlearn all their old tricks. The interesting thing is that the men who make you do crazy things are not necessarily Robert Redford types. They don't have to be rich, successful, or good looking. Women report doing crazy things to get the corner gas station attendant.

The main reason these kinds of crazy tricks don't work is because any man, no matter how unsophisticated he is, will make plans to leave when you act unbalanced or do out-of-the-ordinary things for him. He may not understand what's going on, but no matter who he is, he doesn't want to fall in love with a crazy woman who does crazy things with men. The Love Plan is the sane way to get a man and make him stay.

If you've been in love a lot before, and it has rarely lasted more than six months to two years, you may have been involved in crazy love. The Love Plan will get you into sane love. What's the difference?

In sane love, there is increasing commitment and emotional security. In crazy love, you are never quite sure of the other person. You wonder if he really loves you. The reason for that is because he returns your love—a little bit. Just enough to keep you hooked. He doesn't tell you to get out of his life, but he never quite returns your love all the way either.

He says things like, "I don't want the responsibilities of a relationship." Or, "I don't want to get involved right now." He may even say, "I love you," but you know he only means it if you don't make any demands on him.

He sometimes calls and sometimes doesn't. He's late a lot. Sometimes he doesn't show at all. And all the time, you keep hoping to get your love returned fully.

You fantasize about him belonging just to you. About possessing him. About him loving you more than anyone else in the world. You think about him all the time and may actually enjoy the relationship more when you're apart than when you're together.

He leads you on, just a little. You're happy and then you're sad, depending on what love pellets he throws your way. He seems determined to increase your insecurity, to keep you on edge in the relationship. You wonder how he does it. Maybe secretly, you feel like you've been a fool.

Crazy Love is crazy because it's unbalanced to begin with—you are capable of love and he's not. The more you give of yourself to make him love you, the less he gives. The less he gives, the more desperate you get. The very first step in The Love Plan is to recognize Crazy Love and to understand why it's unhealthy and hopeless.

By the time you finish learning The Love Plan, you will know how to keep Crazy Love out of your life. You'll waste a lot less time in hopeless relationships. Naturally, hopeless men have a lot to do with hopeless relationships. In the next chapter, you will learn how to identify the crazy-making types of men, and how to avoid them.

Breaking Out of "The Bastard Trap"

2

IF YOU'VE HAD A FEW UNSUCCESSFUL RELATIONSHIPS with men who wound up treating you badly, you've probably experienced Crazy Love. You may have even added to the insanity of a go-nowhere relationship. But that doesn't mean that you're incapable of sane love. You may be in The Bastard Trap.

If you've had a *lot* of these experiences, you may be really stuck in The Bastard Trap. You may be a bit cynical. You may feel that *all* men are bastards, but that just is not so. If you've had an unbroken string of bastards, now is the time to take stock. You may have a fatal fascination for bastards. You may not really be ready for a committed relationship. You may be picking the wrong men or you may be "teaching" perfectly okay men to act like bastards—without even knowing you're doing it.

The Bastard Trap is one of the hardest to break out of. The first step is to admit to yourself that there *are* nice guys out there, guys who are open to and capable of giving real love—and vulnerable too, like you, capable of being hurt. There is nothing wrong with falling in love with a nice guy. You don't have to pick ready-made losers if you can spot them ahead of time.

Almost every woman gets involved with at least one bastard in her life. She may marry him, live with him, or just "go" with the jerk. But when it's over she's a basket case and always swears she'll never get involved with a creep like that again.

Some find a nice guy after one run-in with a destructive-type male. Others just keep finding that same no-goodnik over and over again.

Women who get involved with bastards have one thing in common—they all say they didn't know he was like that. "He was so nice in the beginning," she always says. "How was I to know?" Then she cries.

First Signs

I've been involved with a couple of bastards. They're always charming in the beginning; that's how they get you hooked. But once a bastard has you, it's all over.

Almost instantly he starts trying hard to see how much he can get away with. And poor you, you're so in love with his "good" side that you begin to put up with his bad side, just to get close enough for all those wonderful goodies.

You don't say anything when he arrives two hours late for a date. So, of course, he pushes a little further. Soon, he begins to break dates, even if it leaves you stuck with expensive concert tickets.

"I can't help myself," one woman told me about her bastard. "He's so good in bed. He turns me on like nobody ever did. He's the world's best lover."

Of course he is. He's had lots of practice. If he weren't good in bed, he wouldn't get as far as he does. Women wouldn't put up with so much from him if they didn't have a superorgasm to remember him by.

Bastards Are Sexy

Bastards are always sexy—one way or another. "There's a thrill about a guy who may turn nasty," another woman told me. "It's a part of the roller-coaster ride of being in love with him."

Sure, bastards can be exciting. They offer a wealth of emotional problems, like angry former girlfriends who want to kill them, or Mafialike bill collectors, or even the excitement of not knowing if they're going to show up for a date.

Who are these guys? I'll describe a few you might look out for.

How do I know about them? One reason I was single so long is that I picked impossible men, men who couldn't make a commitment, who were too wrapped up in their own trip.

If he was a normal guy with a steady job who wanted a wife and family, I was bored. The ones who turned me on, who made my stomach knot with anticipation and my insides yearn for completion were like the classic tragic heros of Greek drama with at least one fatal flaw that doomed us to eternal separation.

In my twenty years of dating, I suppose I averaged twenty new dates a year. Of those men, fewer than ten percent made a significant contribution to my life and happiness. Maybe eighty percent were men I only dated once or twice; some of these became nonlover friends. The remaining ten percent or so (I hate to admit how many that adds up to) were a complete rogue's gallery of bastards—and I managed to get involved with them all.

Of course, other than married men who pretend they're single, alcoholics and heroin addicts, bastards don't walk around with labels on their foreheads. Being able to spot them ahead of time is hard unless you've had lots of practice. My experience can save you some of this "practice." Part of The Love Plan is learning how to spot and avoid certain universal types of impossible men. So you won't use The Love Plan on the wrong person, always beware of the following—the Terrible Ten!

Ten Classic Bastard Types

1. The Achiever

The Achiever is a universal man married to a higher cause, dedicated to something larger than he is, like medicine, or humanity. The Achiever is an admirable member of society but a lousy partner in a relationship. He pays little attention to you and is often too tired to do anything but sleep when he takes time off.

Your love for each other is a grain of sand compared to the global grandeur of his more time-consuming passion, but he does have some advantages. He is dependable—for some things. He always knows what time it is, he makes dates well in advance, and if he can't show, he'll either call or be reasonably apologetic.

But forget about leisurely time spent just being together. He doesn't have any. He always falls asleep immediately after making love, if he doesn't fall asleep *without* making love. Don't worry about making breakfast in the morning, because he's already gone.

It's easy to get sucked in by an Achiever. On the surface he's such a good citizen, so attractive, successful, hard working, affluent, even intelligent. He's the man your mother always dreamed you'd marry.

It's impossible not to think of marriage with him, because an Achiever offers financial security and obviously needs a wife. Then he could devote more time to his coma patients or to his study of prehistoric reptiles. Without having to worry about details like cooking or cleaning house, he could save precious seconds. Actually, a robot would do if she looked good. He needs someone to sit quietly at awards dinners.

If you try to get him away from his work, he will only make you feel tacky and small. Your world consciousness will be suspect and he'll most likely suggest volunteer work of some kind. If all this upsets you, don't complain to your mother or your friends; they'll agree with him.

The Achiever is universally admired, but when it

comes to returning love, he's a bastard. If you don't want to spend your life as a lonely Stepford wife, don't even start to get involved with this guy.

2. THE GURU

The Guru always has a cause. Often, he's been married and didn't like it, so his higher consciousness tells him that the two of you are above such mundane concerns. He's also a nonbeliever about making money, ironing clothes, eating meals, drinking coffee, high-heeled shoes, makeup, hair coloring, television, psychiatry, organized religion, sports, or anything else that has kept you sane over the years.

Naturally you're suspicious when you first meet a man with a fanatic glow in his eyes, and a deep concern for your "psychic energy," but there's something charming and disarming about his open easy ways. He knows your inner soul. He exudes love. His eye contact is instant and astonishing. Your eyes meet, and his seem to penetrate your innermost secrets.

I was always amazed at how quickly I could be seduced by a Guru. It was the way he cared about my inner void. He was full of ideas to fill it.

The Guru is often a leader with lots of followers who all do exactly what he says. To ensure his continued exalted position you must become one of his followers too, worshipping at the shrine of his latest cause and heeding his every instruction.

He may be involved in est, TM, a new business scheme or multi-level sales. Whatever it is, he expects you to devote your time and assets to his newest cause. There will be lots of people around to hang on his every word. You will be expected to adore him as they do, to do his bidding instantly and to entertain and feed, even to love, his followers as much as you do him.

The Guru is a terrific lover because he thinks he's God doing "it" in his own special way to a disciple, you. He wants to make sure you never forget his greatness.

Once you are fully indoctrinated, agreeing to turn your home and possessions over to him and his entourage and to devote your life to his cause, he really starts dancing on your devotion. "Why do you always follow me around that way?" he wants to know.

The best way to get rid of him is to refuse to let him have meetings at your house.

3. THE TIMEBOMB

The Timebomb is your classic unstable personality hidden beneath a normal veneer. Timebombs come in several varieties—latent alcoholics, compulsive gamblers, obsessive Don Juans, drug abusers, physical abusers, and just plain crazies. If you could see the inner person, you wouldn't go near him. The problem is that the Timebomb is attractive and charming on the surface, and it's hard to hear the Timebomb ticking. . . .

He's so nice in the beginning that you tend to get hooked. Then, just as you begin to feel certain that true love has at last felled you and someone else at the same time, an explosion invariably rocks your security with a Timebomb. And of course the first time it happens you don't recognize it as a pattern.

Afterwards, he swears he is reformed; he'll never

binge, gamble, cheat, O.D., hit you, or go crazy again. . . . If he's got you hooked, you keep loving him, you forgive him, and soon the two of you are together again.

But the signs were there all along. His ex-wife doesn't speak to him, his former live-in girl friend is in an institution for the mentally disturbed, and a jealous male or female is always trying to get him. He hates his job as a salesman and always wanted to be an actor. He even took lessons once.

If you listen closely, he'll give you clues. A Timebomb seems to enjoy telling about his perilous personal life: how his ex-wife tried to run him over with her car, how some guy tried to shoot him for dating his girl.

The Timebomb doesn't just get mad when you argue. He breaks your jaw. He doesn't just fall in love with another woman. He falls in love with your best friend when you're seven months pregnant. He doesn't just lose his job, he gets fired for embezzling money and expects you to stand by him during the trial. He doesn't just blow money at the track, he loses *your* life savings.

Staying with a Timebomb is like flying in an airplane when the pilot's number is up. The temptation to hang around and wait for your beautiful romance to bloom once more can be seductive, but you'd be better off trading parachutes while sky diving.

The Timebomb is seriously disturbed, almost always self-destructive, and sometimes very dangerous. If you've got a Timebomb in your life, accept that his life pattern is unchangeable. If you don't get away, it'll be yours too.

Divide up your mutual possessions and separate your bank accounts first. Then change the locks on your door and your phone number. Never accept collect calls from jail.

4. The Waffler

The Waffler won't make a decision. He's not sure of anything, including whether he wants you. One reason he can't decide is because he's greedy. He really wants everything. He's afraid he's missing something with someone else each minute he's with you.

A Waffler never makes a date ahead of time for anything because he is afraid something better might come along at the last minute, and then he'd be committed to you and unhappy all night thinking about what he might have missed. He breaks dates often, especially after the initial glow of a relationship is fading. You always know it's because he thinks he might get something better. He never stops looking, even after he's been married for years.

There's no real fun in a relationship with a Waffler because he's never satisfied with anything. He can't enjoy the here and now, because he's always imagining a prettier face, bigger tits, a taller, longer-legged version of you somewhere. No real woman ever lives up to the fantasy one in his mind.

A Waffler can change his philosophy of life in an hour; he considers changing careers, homes, selling out and moving away. Nothing he already has is ever any good for very long. He thinks that more or different or new acquisitions will make him happy.

What he really needs is about two years of intensive professional help, not you.

5. The Supervisor

The Supervisor is a natural critic and speaks only from his own perfection. He rarely works, preferring to tell other people what to do. When you meet him, he immediately gives you all his credits, and lets you know you're very lucky he's chosen you.

Naturally, you're impressed by his good taste. It's obvious from the way he criticizes everyone else that you're the perfect two. If it isn't obvious, he tells you. He knows how you should dress, put your makeup on, even brush your teeth, and as long as you agree, he's happy.

He knows what will make *you* happy too! He will direct your career, tell you how to talk to your mother, even what you want in lovemaking. He knows without a doubt that what you really need the most is him.

There's always a moment when things start to go sour in a relationship with a Supervisor: when he discovers you don't dust the tops of the doors. The first chink in your perfection is his opening. From there he splits your self-confidence apart, leaving your ego in little pieces.

Suddenly you can't do simple things you always did almost automatically. If you make coffee, the pot burns up. If it's a roast, it's still frozen on the inside. There's no way you can do anything right.

It's all down from there. Soon the slightest infraction of the Supervisor's rules of conduct turns him into a raging beast and you into a tear-dripping mess.

Strong defiance is the best way to get rid of a Supervisor. Wear the red dress he hates. *Don't* tell your best friend you can't talk on the phone when he's there. Make plans with friends he doesn't like.

6. The Carpetbagger

The Carpetbagger is easy to spot because he arrived at your house and just stays. He doesn't have to call home because he doesn't have one. He always has enough clothes with him to last at least a month. His dog is in the car and so are most of his belongings. He is always broke and hungry when he gets to your house and will stay as long as you feed him and give him lots of love. He's attractive and sweet and helpful around the house and a wonderful lover. He has a way of just fitting in.

But he never takes you anywhere. He's either about to make a fortune or has just lost one. He expects to be nurtured between fortunes.

No matter how much you give the Carpetbagger, he doesn't give anything back, except playing the guitar and making love. When you think he's gotten everything you have to offer, eaten all the food in the house, finished the wine, exhausted you, he'll say, "I have a load of dirty clothes in the trunk of my car. Is it okay if I just put them in your machine?" Then he needs dogfood for his Great Dane, stationery to write his mother, a stamp of course, and do you have a sweater big enough for him to borrow?

In the beginning the Carpetbagger can be tender and delicate with his lovemaking, almost worshipful, a wellspring of foreplay. But when he finishes with lovemaking he usually finds something urgent he must do, leaving you with a foretaste of his ultimate splitting.

When he's around, he's romantic and attentive, and you miss both when he's gone, but he's really a bad bet for a long-term relationship.

You can get rid of the Carpetbagger easily enough by either cutting off his support system or asking for a month's contribution to food and rent in advance. It's always sad when he's gone, though, because he's been around all the time. Without him, your house feels empty, as though your favorite guppy passed away.

7. THE DEALER

The Dealer's real ambition in life is to be invited to join the Corleone family. He has a suicidal fascination with ill-gotten gains and a phobia about honest work. He's not hard to spot, but he has that "Ladies Love Outlaws" kind of appeal.

Somehow he makes you yearn to be taken into his confidence. Besides, you're naturally curious. You can't wait to know all about his shady friends. It's clear that when he admits his criminal dealings to you, you should be flattered. You've earned his sacred trust.

The next step after trust is involvement. He even offers you a profit. All you have to do is let him leave three-hundred pounds of marijuana in your attic for a couple of weeks. Or go on a stolen credit card shopping spree with him. You're perfectly safe, he insists.

Even if you don't get arrested, you soon find that your nerves aren't holding you together the way they used to—before you met the Dealer. Maybe it was because he showed you all his scars and broken bones, or he brought a gun to your apartment, or you think your phone is being tapped by the CIA, but you're taking three Valium a day and still shaking soon after your first date.

If you hang in—for the excitement, the sex, or whatever—it gets worse. Soon he starts treating you like his moll. You and whatever you own are now his possessions. The easiest way to get rid of him is to admit you think the police are watching your house.

8. The Patient

The Patient really wants you to take care of him. His mother wasn't very warm or loving and he is still looking for the woman who will make up for her inadequacies. There is absolutely nothing he won't do to exploit your motherly instincts.

Just your basic sympathy sponge, Patients have been known to fake illness so well that they really make themselves sick. You, Florence Nightingale, are supposed to stand by, ever ready to hold his head at the crucial moment, pluck his ingrown toenail at just the perfect place or soothe his sunburn. There's no limit to the illnesses he can conjure up or inflict on himself.

You can guarantee the Patient will have an abominable toothache in the middle of your birthday party. It seems as if you're always rushing him to some emergency hospital or other. Each new catastrophe requires a new, healthy diet, different vitamins, and the most sincere concern for the funnel functions of his body.

He is grateful for every bit of solicitude and wrings it out of you, sopping it up like mother's milk. You are expected to interrupt anything should his fragile condition require attention. And, of course, this includes sexual ministrations, so you give in every time.

Patients make so much noise when they have an orgasm you think they're going to die. Afterward, instead of tender words whispered softly, from him you get deep rasping noises as he flings himself across the bed and clutches his chest. You always pray he doesn't die on top of you.

You can discourage the Patient by hiding all the medications in your house, even aspirin. Tell him you're a believer in faith healing and that if he wants to get well his mind will cure him. Don't refill the Band-Aids when he uses up the last ones. The next time you hear his agonized yell of pain, say you'll be there when you finish meditating. Complain of various lurid female problems that you think might be contagious. Make him sick enough to check into a hospital by continually telling him how bad he looks.

9. The Cripple

The Cripple is one of the walking wounded in our modern society. Just divorced, he's an emotional basket case. He lives in a large singles' complex with a "ready-renter's" package of plastic plates, tin silverware, and Army surplus cups. His finished studio apartment doesn't have a book or personal picture in sight. It's devoid of healthy emotions, personality, or commitment—just like him.

The Cripple will probably get better, but it may take years. It's certain that you don't want to be the *first* woman he gets involved with after his divorce.

He's still bleeding and too involved with his own pain and losses to make a good mate for you.

He's worried about his ex-wife, the guy she's sleeping with, what her lawyer's taking away from him, the house he already lost, the kids he doesn't know if he'll be able to keep seeing, and how he's going to make those alimony and child-support payments.

For sure, she took something personal of his that he wants back, maybe a whole slew of things.

He's worried about his barbecue he had "before the marriage" twenty years ago, or the plaster monkey he won in a softball tournament, or his tool box that his ex is letting someone else use. He wants his things back more than he wants a relationship with you or anyone else.

Sex with a Cripple is usually a disaster. He can't get it up. Or if he does, he can't keep it up. Or if he keeps it up and actually manages to penetrate you, he can't come. Or if he comes, he feels guilty right afterward.

The way to get rid of the Cripple is to refuse to listen to any more stories about his ex-wife, his divorce, what he lost, his kids, or his past. Refuse to sympathize or help him get the barbecue back. Tell him you think his ex was a very lovely person.

10. The Fairy Godfather

The Fairy Godfather is the one type of bastard who's almost impossible to resist. His pitch is that he's not like all those other men who weren't so nice. He's different, and he's here to show you what real love is like. "Just give me a chance," he begs.

Whatever your secret fantasy is, the Fairy Godfather ferrets it out. He wants to make you happy, so he pretends to be whatever you always wanted. He promises to make your dreams come true, even before he knows specifics. He loves you, loves you, loves you!

He never takes his eyes or his hands off you. Even if there's something obviously wrong with the man, you pretend he's okay because, after all, he does love you and that's good for something.

In almost no time at all, he's like a member of your family. Your parents always ask how he is. They too believe your Fairy Godfather is going to protect you from the world. Lucky you.

Whatever your dreams—marriage, career, a family, travel—the Fairy Godfather is here to make them true. He not only makes dates in advance, he has wonderful things scheduled for the rest of your life.

These fantasy promises the Fairy Godfather dangles in front of you are like a golden carrot, and like a tired racehorse you perk up at the bait. Soon, the thought of losing him is inextricably tied to the thought of losing all your dreams, of never getting to do all the wonderful things he has planned for you. You see houses, trips, true love, marriage, babies, floating away with his love, and so you battle to keep your affair going.

It's a losing fight. The Fairy Godfather is a fantasy (partly yours) and his promises are worth less than the paper they're not written on. You finally begin to notice that nothing you both talk about ever actually *happens.*

The best thing to do at that point is simply realize

it's over, stop looking at him with stardust in your eyes, and he'll go away by himself.

First Aid for Bastard Sufferers

Realistically, nobody's going to hand you your dreams. You're going to have to make them come true on your own. In the next chapter you will learn to develop your own personal "Man Plan," which will help you focus on promising men in the future. If your list of unpromising men is as long as mine, you probably can add some bastard types of your own.

In the meantime, if you're like millions of other women (and the way I was), you may need immediate help in dealing with the men already in your life. What if the guy you're dating isn't exactly one of the ten "Classic" types, but you suspect he's a bastard nevertheless? Are there some quick rules of thumb to identify bastards in general? Is there a damage-limitation strategy you can use while you're finding out?

Of course. The Love Plan puts you more in control of your love life right away, with some common sense rules.

Bastard Checklist

1. First, never go out with someone blindly and assume he's perfect until events prove otherwise. Enjoy being with him, but if you're planning to see him again, start checking him out.

2. Is he an honest person? Does he lie to other people? (If so, chances are he'll lie to you.)

3. Is he responsible? Does he take care of his plants, his pets, his children?

4. Does he have lots of old friends? What do they say about him?

5. Does he seem financially stable? Does he pay his bills? Does he borrow money a lot? Does he gamble? Is he wildly extravagant? Does he drink too much? Does he need drugs all the time?

6. Have you ever felt physically threatened by him?

7. Does he stay friends with his ex-lovers and/or ex-wives?

8. Does he show up when he says he will—or call if he can't?

9. Could you count on him to be there if you needed him?

If a lot of these checklist questions (particularly being physically threatened) are turning up the wrong answers, dump him fast—even if you're lonely and he's all you have right now. In fact, *especially* if you're lonely and he's all you have right now, dump him *immediately,* before you really get hurt.

But what if he only looks ominous on one or two counts? What if you suspect he's a bastard, but it's just too early to tell? Should you still chuck him immediately? Maybe not. He might be worth exploring a little—but you will have to know the technique for handling him.

Bastard Survival Strategy

Some bastards do actually settle down and become devoted husbands and lovers, but only if a woman has enough self-esteem to risk losing the relationship at the first sign of his bad behavior. For example, it's your second date. Your first one was terrific and you're all excited. However, instead of taking you out as you planned to dinner and the theatre, he wants to go right home to bed. No dinner, no theatre, no nothing.

You think to yourself, "So what? I really like this guy. Why not go right home to bed with him? Maybe we'll eat later." So, with mild misgivings, you say okay, and of course, he's terrific in bed. You think, "That was fun, even if it wasn't what we'd planned. Maybe I'll lose weight."

He thinks, "Boy, have I got her signed, sealed and delivered. She'll do anything for me." Next he doesn't call when he says he will, or he shows up unexpectedly. You put up with it because "he's so sexy," or whatever.

The next date, he shows up with a cute little number for a *ménage à trois.* You go bonkers and ask him what made him think he could get away with a thing like that.

The answer is *you* did. You made him think you would put up with anything by not speaking up the first time he got out of line. You should have said, "Hey, I'm hot for you too—but I'm *hungry.* I was looking forward to dinner and a show." Instead you *taught* him to push you around.

Men who've gotten away with treating women badly for a long time just can't help trying the same thing with you. You *might* be able to make him treat you differently, but only if you put your foot down the very first time he does *anything* out of line.

You *must* follow this strategy, even if you don't really care that much whether you go to dinner or the theatre, or whether he calls exactly when he says he will, or whether he stops by unexpectedly. The point is, you can't let a bastard get away with anything, not even once, or you're in trouble.

An interesting thing about this strategy is that it's self-resolving. If he's only an incipient, borderline bastard, he'll be apologetic (and maybe even appreciative) if you challenge him. On the other hand, if he's a dyed-in-the-wool, hopeless bastard, and you don't put up with any of it, he'll treat you better or he'll be gone before he does you any serious damage.

If you've faced lots of these problem men, if you suspect that random dating isn't the best way to find "Mr. Right," the next chapter will get you started on the right foot.

Your Personal "Man Plan"

3

FROM HERE ON, THE LOVE PLAN MUST BE FOLlowed exactly. To do this you have to forget everything else you have ever learned about making a man fall in love with you. The Love Plan will be your step-by-step guide to love.

By following The Love Plan exactly you will be successful just as all the others have before you. No one who has used The Love Plan system has failed to make the man they want fall in love with them. The caveat is that you must be careful on whom you use The Love Plan—you could wind up with the wrong man too much in love with you. Your personal "Man Plan" will help make sure you find the man who is right for *you.*

Be careful, though. You will be tempted to do the

things you did before. To make crazy phone calls, to blurt things out without thinking, to lay your heart on the bed with your body, to let yourself fall for someone you know is a classic bastard, hoping The Love Plan techniques will bail you out.

That's not the way it's done. Stick to the Plan the way you would a diet. Don't cheat. Don't skip parts. Don't deviate, and you too will soon have the man who's right for you in love with you.

Once you have mastered The Love Plan, it will work for you. The Plan doesn't depend on your looks. If you can think and follow instructions, The Love Plan will show you how to find love.

Whoops! There is no man in your life right now, nobody you want to have fall in love with you? Then you need a plan more than ever.

The women who tell you they never "did anything" to get their man, that true love just happened, probably have forgotten their scheming and manipulations—or they were very, very lucky. Getting the right man is just like anything else worthwhile—a good career, financial security, or even good health and a good figure—most of us have to *work* at it.

The next step in The Love Plan is to create your own personal Man Plan. Your Man Plan will set specific goals, help you visualize the man you want and greatly improve your chances of finding him.

Even if you think you already know exactly what you want in a man, a written Man Plan is important. If you know everything about the man you want, completing this chapter will take you very little time and you will feel good about having your instincts confirmed. On the other hand, if you feel unsure who you really want, this chapter will help bring "Mr. Right" into focus. You'll also be surprised at how much you learn about yourself.

If you're already dating a man you're sure you want to spend the rest of your life with, then skip to Chapter Five and go for it! Otherwise, slow down. Take a break in your socializing.

Make a date with yourself some evening this week to start your Man Plan. Buy yourself a special notebook for this purpose and no other. Fix yourself something you enjoy for dinner, have a glass of wine if you like, put on your favorite music, and let's have fun finding out who's right for *you.*

To begin with, many women make the mistake of thinking that they can choose a man from all the available men in the world. That simply isn't true. If you think about it for a while, you'll realize that there are things you don't like about at least fifty percent of the male population.

Your Requirements

Whether you've analyzed it or not, you have specific *requirements* for a man. The older you are, the more requirements you are likely to have. Do you know what you really want in a man? The Man Plan will help you figure it out.

The Man Plan is a profile you will write about the man of your dreams. It will be revised as you use it and think about it, but I want you to begin with your first, honest impulses—just as they come to you. Don't worry if they seem jumbled or even contradictory in the beginning. They will sort themselves out as you go along. The important thing is to *start.*

Don't be shy. Remember, your Man Plan is for your eyes only, like a diary.

Think about how intelligent this man must be. Does he have a college degree or is he just instinctively smart, or street smart, or self-taught? Does he work with his hands? Does he travel in his work? Does he read a lot? What are his favorite books? Hobbies?

Imagine your life together. Where will you live? His place? Your place? A new place for both of you? In the city or the country? Will you work full time? Will you have children together? Remember, if you can't visualize yourself doing something, chances of your accomplishing that thing are slim.

Visualizing

The best way to start to get the man you want is to visualize yourself having him. But you must write it down. Your description of your ideal man can be anywhere from simply filling out the form on page 28 to really going into depth in essay form about what *he'll* be like.

Your Man Plan should be specific, just like any goal planning. It will help you to visualize the man you really want and then, amazingly, you will find him. Visualizing the man you want works very much like visualizing the figure you want when you're on a diet. It helps to have a specific goal to work toward.

Your Man Plan should include physical characteristics of your ideal man. For instance, is he tall or short, slight of build, or big and muscular?

A very tiny woman of less than five feet tall told

me, "I really hate little men. I don't like skinny men either. I need a man I can curl up to, a warm-bodied guy with lots of flesh, a big man who makes me feel protected."

An athletic woman told me, "I can't stand soft flabby men. I want a man who's hard all over, with lots of body hair and muscles. I hate men who are sickly pale. I want a healthy, suntanned guy."

Be honest, isn't there some type of man *you* prefer? If you're not sure, look at the men in your past who turned you on. Did they all have a feature in common? If you can't put your finger on your type of man, ask your close friends what they have observed. They may have a clearer impression than you do about what types of men you have always found attractive.

There's nothing wrong with physical types attracting you. After all, for years men have been attracted to "leggy blondes" or "petite brunettes." You're just as entitled to a physical type that turns you on.

Describe your dream man in every detail. How tall is he? How much does he weigh? How old is he? Is he hairy? Is he circumcised? Is he muscular or tall and thin? What color is his hair? What color are his eyes? What do his hands look like? Does he have a manicure? Does he have a bald spot?

Next, his personality. Is he an athlete? A sedentary type? Is he sensitive and warm? Is he outgoing? Is he an introvert? Is he the quiet type, or is he the life of a party? Does he like to stay at home or go out dancing? What kind of music does he like? What kind of music would he never play? Does he watch television? Does he drink? Does he smoke cigarettes? Does he do drugs? Marijuana? Coke?

What does he talk about? Politics? Religion? Sports? Music? Movies? Love? Relationships?

What's important to him? His career? His home? His love life? In what order?

What does he do for a living? Does he go to work in a three-piece suit every day, or is he an artist who works at home?

Does he like animals? Does he have children? Does he want children? Does he have children living with him?

Has he been married before? How many times?

Is he religious? Does he go to church regularly?

In making your Man Plan, you'll be surprised to find out that you do indeed have a particular man in mind. You really do have requirements of your own. If you're having trouble getting started on a personal Man Plan, start by filling in your personal Man Plan on the following pages.

It is important that you have a clear picture of the man you want. That's the first step toward finding him. Your Man Plan starts with personal affirmations, strong "I" statements that act as reinforcements in your mind. Say the affirmations out loud.

If you have trouble saying them, that could be a sign that you don't believe you deserve the good things a healthy love relationship can bring. Practice the affirmations until you can say them without feeling strange.

Many women are kept from finding true love because they refuse to admit that's what they want.

Affirmations will help erase old programming that can keep you from finding your man.

I asked one woman friend with very specific requirements if I could borrow her "first draft" Man Plan to use as an example. She is now happily married, but at the time she wrote this, she thought she'd never find anyone. She has muscular dystrophy, so she had some special requirements.

Sample Man Plan

My man is Caucasian, 35–50 years old, 6′1″ tall, 160–195 pounds. On a scale of one to ten, he is a seven to ten. We are a good fit, sexually. He is hung, big around but not too long.

He is strong and healthy and able to accept my health problems and love me as I am. He doesn't want any more children. His children from a former marriage aren't living with him. They will visit us occasionally, but I won't have to mother them.

He is spiritual, affectionate, demonstrative, and touchy, literate and educated. He is sophisticated, but not a snob. He is an architect, a lawyer, a doctor, an artist, or an entrepreneur.

We go out to cultural events and live in beautiful surroundings. He has a scientific background. Politically he is a little right of center.

He takes pride in his appearance. If he's balding, he'll have a good toupee. He's interested in physical fitness and diet and he doesn't smoke *anything.* He drinks occasionally but not every night. He never uses drugs.

He wants to have sex all the time. He's a sophisticated lover who can enjoy giving and receiving oral sex. He sees sex as a way of sharing intimacy. He can be playful during sex and often keeps his erection for a half hour or more.

He tells me he loves me all the time. Often he says how beautiful I am and what a wonderful person I am.

He's an extrovert and likes animals, but he loves me the most of anyone or anything.

He's reliable. If he says he's going to do something he does it. I trust him and he trusts me, but we have a prenuptial agreement. What's mine is mine and what's his is his.

Most important, he's the one who pursues me. He calls me. I'm not the one who wants him to marry me. He asks me to marry him.

AFFIRMATIONS
(To Say Out Loud)

I, (first name) (last name), am about to find the man I want.

I, ____________ ____________, deserve all the love I am entitled to, and I will find it soon.

I, ____________ ____________, am about to have a wonderful loving relationship with a man who really loves me as much as I love him.

Man-Plan Physical Description

He is ________ tall. He has ________ eyes, ________ hair. He is ________ years old. He has a ________ build.

PERSONAL MAN PLAN
(To Write Yourself)

Finances and Job

He feels ________ about his work. He is in the ________ business. He is ________ creative. His work is ________ important to him. Success is ________ important to him. He makes ________ a year. He has a (conservative), (relaxed) approach to money matters. I ________ continue to work as a ________. His work takes him out of town (sometimes), (never), (often).

Politics

He is a political (liberal), (conservative). He votes ________. He is politically (active), (inactive).

Religion

He is a (practicing), (nonpracticing) ________. He goes to (church), (synagogue), (other). He goes to a religious service (sometimes), (regularly), (often).

Marital History

He ________ been married before. He has ________ ex-wives. They live (far away), (close by). He (is) (isn't) friends with them.

Children

He has ________ children. They live (with their mother), (with him). He sees them every ________. He wants ________ children. He (enjoys), (could live without) children.

Personal Habits

He dresses in ________ most of the time. He is a ________ dresser. He enjoys (staying home), (going dancing). He drinks ________. He (is), (isn't) a smoker. He ________ use recreational drugs. He spends ________ time alone. He spends ________ time with his male friends.

Hobbies

He (is), (isn't) athletic and plays in sports (rarely), (often). His favorite sport is ________. He also likes to ________ (hunt, fish, etc.). On Sunday afternoons, he likes to ________ (watch ball games, go for a drive, etc.)

He (is), (isn't) the intellectual type and prefers to (stay home and read), (work with his computer), (go dancing), (work in the garden). Music (is), (isn't) important to him.

He (does), (doesn't) enjoy pets.

Personality Type

He is (sensitive and caring), (a helper type), (a rugged individualist), or

He (does), (doesn't) put other people first.

NOTE

Don't be shy about your requirements. They're only guidelines and will change as you date.

Demanding? Difficult? Inconsistent? Different from what you'd want? That's the point.

Your Man Plan is for *you*—it's individual, intentionally selfish and private, like a secret diary.

Remember, this was my friend's very first attempt at a Man Plan. Naturally, it changed. It became more flexible, more realistic as she used it—and for the first time in her life, she felt like she wasn't blindly groping. Her interest in men became focused and her dating was goal oriented.

Her Man Plan worked. She avoided a lot of guys who were hopelessly incompatible, and the man she married is a lot like her original requirements.

Your Man Plan will change as you refine it. For instance, starting out you may think that you must have a very rich man to make you happy. You begin dating a man you like a lot and he doesn't have that much money, but you find money is not really so important to you.

You may have a Man Plan that calls for an athlete, or a lawyer, or a doctor, and you may find out that's not what you want at all. If you meet someone you are very much attracted to and he doesn't match your Man Plan, you should either revise your Man Plan, or start looking for someone else. Don't fudge. If you follow this procedure, you will be making rational decisions about what is really important to you in a man—and you will be steadily "homing in" on Mr. Right.

It was no accident that I found the man of my dreams. I made a Man Plan and I revised it over and over again until I had it right. With each man I dated, I changed my requirements, adding some, taking away others. It took several months to refine my plan, making changes sometimes two or three times a week.

Qualifiers

As my Man Plan firmed up, it increasingly helped me to qualify men ahead of time. I found I was saving many valuable evenings instead of wasting time with obviously unsuitable men.

On the other hand, if a new man was a "mismatch" with my Man Plan in a category that was still open to question, I would give the real man the benefit of the doubt and date him. I knew that either the Man Plan was wrong in that category or the man was wrong for me. It never took very long to find out.

When I was dating a new man, I kept my Man Plan in mind and asked myself lots of questions about him. My questions steadily became smarter. One question I started asking earlier and earlier was, "Is he a loner, or has he made commitments in the past?" A man who has *never* made a commitment to a woman before is not likely to change his stripes. I knew my Man Plan required a man who was at least amenable to the idea of a serious commitment. That one question eliminated several men whom I would previously have wasted a lot of time dating.

For example, there was the heir to a large loan-company fortune: rich, tall, handsome, travelled, educated, with a beautiful home just ready for a woman to move in. Unfortunately he was forty-two, never married, and still looking for the right woman.

I wrote him off as a confirmed bachelor in spite of his protestations. I also wrote off all men who made a particular point of not wanting to be involved. Or never wanting to get married. I figured they were telling the truth.

It really isn't very hard to find out how a man feels about making a commitment. Ask him. Simple questions like, "Have you ever been married? In love? Lived with anyone?"

One reason I disqualified men who were "older" bachelors was because I knew I had gotten to be an older bachelorette from a fear of commitment as well as a love of independence. I figured if the guy was a great lover, a terrific looker, rich, kind, or simply decent, more determined women than me with better looks and cuter figures had already tried.

I also checked for a string of broken-hearted women left behind, another bad sign. If a man treated other women badly, he's likely to treat you that way too. If you've been involved in lots of Crazy Love or found yourself in the Bastard Trap (see Chapters One and Two), you may be picking the wrong men and staying with them for the wrong reasons.

I always found out if a man was friends with his exes. If not, it could be because he was so lousy to them they never wanted to hear his name again. If possible, talk to other women who've dated the man you're interested in. Don't be shy, and don't be foolish enough to think every woman is your enemy.

The best recommendations are from ex-wives or ex-lovers. Next come grown children, or even little ones. They know how Dad treats ladies and are often indiscreet enough to tell.

Another good way to judge a man is by finding

out about his parents. Are they still together? Does he love them both? And most importantly, how does his father treat his mother? Little boys first learn how to treat women from watching how their daddies treat their mommies.

Don't just grab the first man who comes along. Follow the next chapter to make sure you are exposed to lots of eligible men. Check each man you meet against your Man Plan. You are going to be strategic from now on. You are going to follow The Love Plan, and you are going to succeed.

Your Search Plan

4

YOU'VE GOT YOUR MAN PLAN AND YOU'RE SURE you're ready for Mr. Right, but you don't have the foggiest notion about how to find him. Worse—you've never been particularly good at meeting men. Relax. The Love Plan will help make it much easier for you. But first, you've got to leave the "Prince Charming" fantasies far behind.

We've all been told there's someone out there for us, our own Prince Charming. And somehow, *he* will find *you*, like Cinderella's prince with the glass slipper. "Someday My Prince Will Come," sang Snow White. Her Prince came, too, and found her sleeping in the forest. Well, Princess, I hate to break it to you, but that only happens in fairy tales.

In the real world, your Prince Charming isn't

wandering around on a white horse just looking for you. More likely, he's on some corporate jet, working around the clock to put a merger together. Or leaving directly from his place of work for a weekend of dirt biking or water skiing with his buddies. So how do you connect?

For starters, *you've* got to do the connecting. The Love Plan will give you magic, but not the kind that places your Prince on your doorstep without you lifting a finger. Princes are hard to find these days, and there are a lot of women out there looking.

The Love Plan will organize your looking and show you how to make him love you, but you must follow the Search Plan. The Search Plan requires that you be willing to make a real *commitment* to the search, and be willing to meet a *volume* of men.

The Commitment

You are looking for the man with whom you will spend the rest of your life. How important is that to you? It should be the third most important thing in your life, after yourself and your work.

The Love Plan requires that you take this search seriously, that you devote as much time to it as you would, say, to night classes and homework if you were going after a law degree.

Without this kind of commitment, those old Prince Charming fairy tales will subtly lull you into hopeful passivity. Even if you're active, really "out there," your searching is probably sporadic and disorganized. Mine always was.

A real commitment to your search will set you apart from all those other women who are looking.

You will conduct an organized, goal-oriented search and you will get to select from a real volume of men.

The Value of "Volume"

Just because you've completed your Man Plan and you think you have a very clear picture of Mr. Right, don't think he's going to be the first man you meet. If you fall for the very first guy who resembles your Man Plan, you won't be getting the full benefit of The Love Plan. Remember, your first-draft Man Plan is just a starting point. It needs to be tested against real men before you can be sure it's right.

The idea is to check out *lots* of men who appear to meet at least some of your Man Plan requirements. You don't have to sleep with all of them, of course, and you don't even have to date all of them—but you must get to know each one well enough to decide whether or not he really does match some of your important Man Plan requirements. If he does, you probably will want to date him, at least once.

Why date lots of men? Several reasons. You will develop self-confidence. You will be able to test and refine your Man Plan. Most important, you will be giving yourself plenty of chances to *compare* men and think about what you're learning. As you do this, you will find yourself becoming steadily more discerning about men, more sure of what you want, and ultimately, free of self-doubt when the time comes to make a commitment.

Once you have made a commitment to your search and understand the importance of volume, you may begin to recognize ways you have cut off certain options. You may have told yourself, "I'd never go out with someone from work," or, "I'd never go on a blind date," or "I'd never join a dating service."

Now is the time to forget your old limits. Leave them behind, with your Prince Charming fantasies.

There are many different ways to meet men. I will give you the pros and cons of some of these, but first you must plan your searching so that you're sure to cover all the bases. Your personal Search Plan must include three different approaches: "open searching," which enlists the help of your friends; a "volume" approach; and your "primary" approach—a spare-time activity that puts you in contact with a certain kind of man.

This combination of approaches is a proven strategy for providing you with a steady supply of interesting new men. Your Man Plan will help you pick out the most promising, and sooner than you think, you will "home in" on Mr. Right. It all starts with being honest with your friends.

Open Searching

Stand up and say, "I'm available and I'm looking." Sometimes pride keeps us from doing this, but it also discourages our friends from thinking of us when an eligible man pops up. Swallow your pride and go ahead. It's already obvious that you're available, and you'll be respected for admitting that you're looking. This approach usually yields high-quality dates, but you can't count on it for volume.

Your Volume Approach

Your personal Search Plan must include an approach that guarantees a sure *volume* of men, together with an efficient way of sorting through them.

The two best examples of the volume approach are classified ads and dating services. Tacky, you think? Maybe so, but you'll certainly be exposed to a wide spectrum of men, and that's an essential part of your search strategy. Remember, this can be your own private endeavor. You don't have to tell anyone, and you don't have to date, or even respond to anyone who doesn't pique your interest. (More on this later.)

Your Primary Search Activity

Since this is where you will be spending most of your searching time, your primary search activity should be something that is educational and/or fun for you.

Finding your primary search activity starts with a thorough review of your Man Plan. If your ideal man happens to be in the same business you are, or in a related line of work, that tells you something. Instead of random dating or sitting at home watching television, you should *immediately* find out about all the organizations and activities related to your (or his) business.

If you're professionally minded, join one of the professional societies or organizations associated with your line of work. These are often national in scope, and if you're active in the organization, you will be in contact with an endless supply of new men.

If you're sports minded, join the company softball or bowling team. If you're not very good at the particular sport involved, offer to learn, or to organize a cheerleading and beer-drinking auxiliary, or to be the team "manager" (avoid "mascot" at all cost).

And what if your ideal man is in a totally different line of work? It's okay to keep your eyes open around the office (more about that later), but your primary search should be elsewhere. And where is Elsewhere? To be smart, the elsewhere you want to concentrate on is an activity that men flock to—and that you can also enjoy. This will probably mean getting out of doors. If you're an indoor person, think about expanding your horizons a little. Isn't there *any* sport you might like?

Have you ever wanted to learn to scuba dive? Classes generally start in a pool. You may meet someone long before you have to face deep water or real fishies.

What about skiing? You can join a club and start meeting men long before you even have to face a slope. Too expensive? Rent equipment and go with a group. Still too expensive, and besides, hills terrify you? Try cross-country skiing. Live hundreds of miles from snow? Find a water-skiing club. The man/woman ratio is almost as good as snow skiing.

Consider flying lessons—a sure way to meet interesting men. Too expensive? Try soaring (glider flying). It's much cheaper, very esthetic, and safer than driving a car. (This is not to be confused with hang-gliding, however, which I'm definitely *not* recommending, not even to find Mr. Right.)

Your primary search requires a real commitment of spare time to either a professional organization or an activity with a favorable man/woman ratio. Since this will be the search activity you spend the most time at, it should also be genuinely enjoyable and worthwhile for you personally.

Specific Ways of Meeting Men

It is up to you to decide on specific activities for open searching, your volume approach, and your primary search activity. To help you decide, here are the pros and cons of many frequently used ways of meeting men. However, *don't feel limited to these.* Be inventive. Apply the principles of the Search Plan to your own situation.

Work

Once fellow workers were definitely off limits. Some companies even had policies that if you were caught co-mingling with another employee, one of you would have to go. Fortunately, most companies have a broader outlook today and many women have found husbands right in their very own offices.

Advantages You get to see another side of the man you're dating. You'll always know where he is and what he's doing during the day.

Disadvantages Privacy will be hard to maintain. Office romances hardly ever stay secret.

The Fix-up

Getting introduced, or fixed-up by friends is one of the best ways to meet men. The way to get friends to introduce you to eligible men is to ask, then ask again. "Don't you know anyone I might like?" is fair. If not this week, maybe the same friend might meet someone next week.

Another way to meet people's eligible man friends is to have a party. Tell them to bring "him" along.

Advantages Your friends know your lifestyle. They have an idea who would be suitable for you. They are familiar with some of the men you've dated in the past. They know your taste and type. Being fixed up by a friend can save you a lot of time, and it's a good double-check on your Man Plan.

Disadvantages Your friend will take a proprietary interest in the relationship, want to know all the details, and feel left out if you don't come clean. Also, your friend may have a "direct line" to the man, which could be a disadvantage or an advantage.

Churches

Don't be shy about meeting at church. There's a certain acceptability to the practice that goes back years. Many churches and synagogues have organizations for singles you can join. Go to the biggest function and check out the men.

Advantages Meeting at church is a terrific idea. Any single man stands out there because if he has a wife she'll be along. It's easy to get information from other parishioners about the man you're interested in. He's indoctrinated to marriage and family.

Disadvantages He probably won't want to get caught staying over at your place or doing any overtly racy acts that could get gossip started.

Singles' Parties

Singles' parties *are* meat markets, and you do have to be strong of heart to survive. If you go with a girlfriend, split up at the door. (It's harder to meet two men than one.) Dance with anybody who asks, even if he's a nerd. On the dance floor you can be seen better than on the sidelines. Sit at a well-lit place. Smile at everyone. Talk to anybody, but don't let a creep trap you. All you have to say is, "Nice meeting you, but I think I'll circulate a bit." Look as if you're having fun.

Advantages Everyone is in the same boat. You don't feel as if you are the only lonely person in the city when you go to one of these events.

Disadvantages At a singles' party you're likely to be judged on your looks rather than your accomplishments or personality.

Classified Ads

Don't be afraid either to advertise or to answer an ad. *Always* meet in a safe public place until you have a chance to check the man out thoroughly. I know lots of women who've used ads to meet interesting men. Advertise in the kind of newspaper or magazine the man you'd like to meet would read.

Advantages You're volume shopping and only choosing the ones you like. You can advertise your best features, leaving out the rest.

Disadvantages You don't know what the person looks like until you actually meet. Even when photos are exchanged they are rarely up to date or even accurate. Men often lie about their age and height.

Dating Clubs

There are some very chic and exclusive private dating clubs in most major cities. They send out a select number of men's profiles to members each month and hold parties.

Advantages You will only meet people who can afford to join such a club. They will be committed to finding a relationship to the tune of many bucks they have spent to join.

Disadvantages The price is often high, up to $1,000 per year. There are so many available members that it's hard to spend enough time with one to see if he's right. There's always the temptation just to go on to someone else.

Video Dating

A high-tech newcomer to the dating scene, video is an efficient way to meet eligible men.

Advantages You never get rejected in person. You get to see and hear a tape before you commit to meet. Also, as in dating clubs, you will only meet men who can afford the service.

Disadvantages The men rarely look or sound in person exactly the way they do on the video tape, but at least you're not "flying blind."

Coed Gyms

There are lots of attractive people working out these days. Regularly stretching, biking, or pumping iron next to a guy is a good way to start conversation. Go when the men work out—either before work in the morning or after work in the evening or on weekends. Learn to play racketball.

Advantages You get to see what a guy really looks like. You will find someone healthy. You'll stay in shape.

Disadvantages He may look better all pumped up and sweaty than he really is. You will have to let it all hang out and will be competing with some very attractive women.

Classes, Clubs, Societies, and Museums

This will be your primary search activity. Since you will be committing a lot of your spare time to this activity, make sure it's something that you will enjoy.

For example, you're almost sure to meet a man on a Sierra Club hike, but of course you have to want to meet a hiker. If you can't decide what sport you want to specialize in, check out various health clubs for the quality of their male patrons. (And it won't do any harm to get in better shape while you're at it.)

On the other hand, if you're dead set against any physical activity, you can still find a primary search activity that will bring you in touch with the right kind of man for you—if you're a little creative. For example, most universities have an adult program offering an astronomy class. Those nighttime field trips to view the constellations can get downright romantic. (Just arrange to car pool with the right classmate.)

Also in the nonathletic category are professional organizations (reviewed above), as well as political campaigns and special-purpose organizations (e.g., Single Parents, Greenpeace, not Zero Population or Gay Lib)—whatever interests you as long as there are some male members.

The point is, get out there, learn something, and have fun. Just make sure you get into something a lot of men are doing, too.

Advantages You can meet a man without ever having to make the admission that you are more interested in meeting someone than in mountain climbing.

Disadvantage He may only be interested in the class, club, or mountain climbing. Or he may be gay. Or he may be married.

The "Cute Meet"

In movies, the "cute meet" is when she rams his Rolls Royce with her old Plymouth. Or they get stuck together in the elevator. Or her horse runs away and he saves her.

Advantages It's the Prince Charming fantasy, updated. If it ever should happen, you *would* have a terrific story to tell people when they ask how you met.

Disadvantages It's the Prince Charming fantasy, a fairytale enhanced by Hollywood. If you wait for it to really happen, you will be the world's oldest bride.

What Do You Say?

I've met very few single women who are totally comfortable meeting a single man for the first time. I've met even *fewer* men who are totally comfortable meeting a single woman for the first time. That's the key to learning how to meet a man.

"Breaking the ice" is an apt old expression. There is an inevitable awkwardness when you first meet a desirable man—even when you "feel" he wants to meet you too. If you simply accept the awkwardness, and understand with confidence that he feels it too, you will bring a little grace to a situation that needs it badly. The man will be grateful and eager to spend more time with you.

Be smart, though. If he's not giving you any special attention at all, or if he seems to be wrapped up in an involving conversation, cool it. Wait until he's looking your way. At that point, there's nothing wrong with a good old-fashioned flirtatious look. If he never returns it at all, it's probably best to look elsewhere. If he returns your look, hold it for a moment, smile a little, and then look down. Then start figuring out what to say to him. Don't wait for him to come to you.

Almost any man is extravagantly flattered if a woman makes the first move. Walk over to him.

You *don't* have to be glib. If you're not naturally extroverted, witty and quick with a response, it's a mistake to try to be cutesy. This is not Burt Reynolds and Sally Field "spontaneously" charming each other for the first time. It's two uncomfortable *real* people in *real* life. So what do you say? Easy. Say something based on what's happening.

If he flirts back at you outrageously, you should already feel confident. Ask him, "How come you're such an outrageous flirt?" If he seems real interested but not very aggressive, use a little self-disclosure. For example, "I seem to find myself looking at you, and I'm not sure I've ever met you. My name is________." Or, "Everybody else seems to be having all the fun, and I don't know anyone here. My name is________, what's yours?"

Actually, any opening line will probably do. If you feel totally uncreative, you can always get away with old creakers like, "What time do you have?" Any man who has flirted back at you will be flattered that you came over to talk to him. That's the easy part.

What you'd best be prepared for is that he'll simply respond to what you said—and then he'll expect you to say something else. Have a second question in mind, related even vaguely to the first. Following up from the above examples, say, "You did remind me of someone, but your voice is totally different. What do you do?" And, "I guess you must know (the hosts). Are you in the same business as Ed?"

Say *anything* to get the conversation past the first question and answer. Remember, he's finding it just as difficult. Once you know his name and you've exchanged a sentence or two, more self-disclosure may be in order. For example, "Oh, I just have the *worst* time meeting people for the first time—and you're so (cute), (intelligent), (popular, etc.). It isn't the same with you, is it?"

That's all you need in order to make contact. The Love Plan will make the rest easy.

Why Men Love: A New Way to Get Close

5

I ONCE SPENT A WEEK UNSUCCESSFULLY TRYING TO "turn a $100 trick" at a glitzy Lake Tahoe casino. I was on a magazine assignment so luckily my lack of talent as a prostitute didn't matter; I just had to write an article about trying. But I was surprised to find out which one of the girls was making the most money.

She was a "Plain Jane" type with a short, blonde, athlete's haircut, a slim boyish figure, and preppy, not terribly sexy clothes. I studied her not-too-terrific features and kept asking all the men what it was about her that was so great. Did she do something wonderful or unusual in bed?

"She's got a great personality," they told me. Watching her, I found she had a special way of being with a man. She sort of fit herself into him, even standing at the bar. I later realized she was one of those lucky women who instinctively knows how to make a man fall in love with her.

It's always amazing to really beautiful women that a rather plain type can drive men crazy with love and desire. Have you ever asked one of these lucky women what it is that makes men love them so much? I have. The answer is usually something like, "I'm really a good listener." Or, "The reason men love me is because I become their best friend." Or, "Men love me because I really love them."

So you're intelligent and you learn to listen, to be a good friend, and you probably love men a lot. That doesn't do you much good if they don't love you back. Now, everything these ladies say is true. Men *do* love them because they listen and are good friends and love men. But those are just pieces of the puzzle.

When you ask the men who fall madly in love with these women, their answers are even more vague, if that's possible. "What can I say? I'm just crazy about her."

My friend Elaine is really beautiful, and successful too. The kind of woman men always look at again. "I can't understand it," she told me, envying her best friend's marriage.

"Robin is thirty, maybe forty pounds overweight, yet Roger acts as though she were the most beautiful woman in the world. He absolutely adores her. He thinks she's super-intelligent and really going to write a great novel some day. I just don't get it. What's she got? I mean she's nice and everything, but how come she's always had men in love with her? Robin's been married twice and I don't seem to be able to get close to a man at all."

For Elaine, who is truly beautiful, her friend Robin's happiness represents an unfairness in the world. Elaine just can't understand why her own relationships are so unsatisfactory, when she works so hard at being attractive to men.

There are some women men will do anything for. Caroline is one of these women. She's always being showered with gifts, big ones like cars and jewels and houses, and there are always lots and lots of men in love with her.

Sometimes her life seems to be like a rerun of the old Somerset Maugham story, *Of Human Bondage,* where some man is so obsessed with his love for a woman that he destroys his life following her around. Other days, it sounds like a modern-day romance novel with Caroline jet setting around the world with different rich attractive men who adore her.

What's so special about Caroline that men would leave wives and children, sacrifice fortunes, and give her anything she wants? Caroline says it's because she really knows how to make a man feel good. So what does that mean? We've all made men feel good, but there are only a few Carolines in the world.

Caroline and Elaine's friend Robin and even the high-earning hooker are among those rare, lucky women who automatically seem to know how to make a man fall in love with them—without consciously knowing what techniques they are using.

Exciting new findings in the psychology of human communication have unlocked the secrets of these love techniques. For the first time, they can now be learned—by anyone. You don't have to be born a Caroline or a Robin. They have worked for me and for everyone who has used them. You will learn them, as the next steps in The Love Plan.

The Chemistry of Love

True love is built on a bridge of communication. Whenever I felt really "in love," I seemed to somehow identify with the inner core of my lover—we were "on the same wavelength." I used to think it was some mysterious chemistry, because I never experienced this special level of communication except when I was in love.

It turns out that the "mysterious chemistry" of love *starts* with being "on the same wavelength." *Then* the chemistry comes. The "chemistry" doesn't come first; being "on the same wavelength" does. This communication between two lovers *is* special and different, just as we always thought. Only now we know why. We know what's special and different about it; we can create it at will. Now, any one of us can *make* the "chemistry" happen.

The special, deep level of communication that causes the "chemistry" occurs whenever two people are relating in the same Love Language.

Everyone perceives his or her world with three basic senses—sight, sound, and feelings. What psychologists have just discovered is that, for every man and woman, one of these senses is dominant to some degree or other. This sense is never dominant to the degree of *excluding* the other senses, but it has a pervasive influence, only recently understood.

A man's primary sense strongly affects his perception of the world. It deeply influences his personality. It determines how he communicates his inner thoughts. It is his "wavelength." Most important, in a man's interaction with a woman, it is his "Love Language."

Knowing a man's Love Language is the key to deep communication with him. He isn't even aware of it, but he is automatically "tuned in" and totally receptive in his particular "language"—sight, sound, or feelings.

The Love Plan will teach you how to detect your man's particular "wavelength" and to understand how he relates to the world around him. After that, it's amazingly easy to talk to him in his Love Language, to make him feel you really understand his inner being.

Just as a few Million Dollar Club salesmen and women intuitively zero in on a customer's wavelength, you will be able to get "in tune" with any man you wish. Even at the very first meeting, with little or no real information about a man, you will learn to establish instant rapport with him. He won't know why, but he will have a feeling that he likes you and wants to know you better.

The First Date

Let's say you've met a new man who appears to fit your personal Man Plan. He's tall enough, rich enough, sensitive enough, smart enough—whatever your particular plan calls for. And he doesn't seem to fit any of the "bastard categories." He has possibilities. You're getting ready to have a first casual lunch date.

Of course, you're filled with questions you think you *must* ask him right away—and things you *must* tell him.

Maybe you're anxious to let him know how well you're doing with your career. Or how you've just broken up with a guy who's a louse. Or how interesting your life is.

Forget it all. At least for right now. The most important thing for you to do on a first date is to find out if your new man is a visual, auditory, or feeling person. You will start to relate to him in that Love Language, and by the end of the date, he'll know he wants to see you again. You will then have the whole rest of the relationship to tell him about yourself.

Naturally you also want to know all about him—more about what he does, his past relationships, or whether he's seeing someone special right now.

You *will* learn all about him. Faster than you've ever learned about anyone before. But you will do so strategically, by following The Love Plan.

You will ask him questions, but in a new way. You will also be watching and listening as The Love Plan prescribes, and you will discover your new man's Love Language as he answers your questions. Then you will start speaking to him in that same language.

As soon as you shift into his Love Language, your new man will suddenly find himself very comfortable with you. Without knowing why, he will feel an easy rapport with you.

Communication, so often strained and guarded in a first encounter, will flow naturally and candidly.

You will "see" inside this man. It will be an exhilarating experience for you. For him, it may be the start of "that old black magic." He will certainly feel a strong desire to see you again.

Missed Connections

Since everyone's Love Language is one of three—sight, sound, or feeling—you do have a random chance of being on the same wavelength as the next man you meet. But without The Love Plan, you will not know for sure; you will not have a confident sense of how to transform that wavelength match into love.

Worse, if you don't just happen to share the same wavelength, you will be talking but he won't be really listening.

A relationship may still develop, but it's hit or miss, with you feeling the old familiar insecurities, the sense of being "so near but yet so far."

With The Love Plan, you will begin to know the man you're with even better than he knows himself. A man's Love Language is the key to his thoughts and the reflection of his soul. Soon you will have that key.

After developing The Love Plan and watching it work, I now find it quite amazing that we can sometimes have extended love relationships with men and never really know how they think. You may have the greatest sex in the world, but if you're not getting close to the soul of the man you're in bed with, the relationship has a dubious future.

Jennifer, an insurance salesperson, just met a man she really liked. He was the owner of an art museum, a collector of antique cars, who always wore terrific-looking suits.

Jennifer told me about one conversation they had during their third (and last) date. Believe it or not, she couldn't understand why he never called her after that.

"He was wonderful in bed, and we were really communicating well," she told me. In fact, the sex may have been all they had. They spoke entirely different languages.

Here's what happened.

Roger and Jennifer spent the day at a *concours d'elegance.* Driving back along the beautiful California coastal route, they enjoyed a spectacular sunset. They cuddled together in the car. She could tell he had enjoyed the day and was in a loving mood.

When they got back to Jennifer's place, they had drinks and were about to go to bed when Jennifer said, "Oh, Roger, I've never felt this way about any man before. You make me feel as if my heart is about to burst. Tell me, don't you feel it too?"

Jennifer felt Roger physically stiffen beside her. "Actually," he coughed, "I don't quite see what you mean."

Jennifer, now alarmed, strained to explain.

"You must know how I feel about you. When I think about you, my heart pounds. I can't help it, I'll die if you don't tell me—are you in love with anyone else? When I think of you being with another woman, I feel like crying." Then she started to weep. "Promise me there's nobody else."

Roger was visibly uncomfortable, but Jennifer wasn't looking at him. She was too busy blowing her nose.

"My picture of a good relationship is a little more casual than that," Roger tried to explain. "I saw us having a more open friendship and of course making love whenever we see an opportunity."

Jennifer really began to cry then.

"Oh, I feel so rejected," she wept. "I should never have told you all those things about how I felt and how I hoped you'd feel. Now you probably despise me and never want to be with me again."

"You're a beautiful woman, and I enjoy seeing you," Roger told her. "Of course I want to see you again."

Naturally she never heard from him again.

Jennifer was certainly right about one thing. She shouldn't have told Roger how she felt, at least not then, not all at once. If she had been following The Love Plan, she would have known that feelings made Roger uncomfortable.

Jennifer would have first found out that Roger was a totally visual man, then talked to him in visual, not feelings, terms. By telling him how much she enjoyed the coastal *view,* how *handsome* he *looked* in his new sweater, and how she could *see* them taking trips up the coast often, she would have been speaking to him in his Love Language.

Discovering His Love Language

Now, back to that first casual lunch date with a new man. In following The Love Plan, you will concentrate on determining your new man's Love Language first thing, so you won't even begin to get into Jennifer's situation.

If he's mentioned a recent business trip, for instance, and you asked him, "How was your trip?" the visual man might answer, "Lousy. I didn't see the sun one day I was gone." The man who experiences his world primarily in a visual mode will tend to tell you how things *looked.*

An auditory man will tend to tell you how things *sounded.* For example, "The business went well, but my room was so noisy I hardly slept."

A feelings man will tend to tell you how things *felt.* He might say, "Actually, I hate travelling; it's always so lonely in strange cities."

Don't expect to get an instant "read" on any man, though. Remember, you're not used to asking these "neutral" kinds of questions that draw out indications of a man's Love Language, and you're new to interpreting the clues in his answers. So, take your time, enjoy the conversation—and just remember to sprinkle it with neutral questions. Really listen when he answers. A pattern will emerge.

Another good question is, "Tell me about your home town." The visual man might answer, "It's a pretty little desert town with big cactus and lots of mountains around it." An auditory man (who also tends to be very logical) might tell you, "It's seventy-five miles northwest of Phoenix, very serene and quiet." A feelings man might say, "It's a very close, tight little community—I kind of miss it sometimes."

Yet another good question is, "I'm thinking about getting a new car. How did you decide on your Ferrari?" The visual man might answer, "It looks like it's doing 120 just standing still." The auditory man might say, "Nothing sounds like a Ferrari—at 8,000 rpm, it just sings." The feelings man might tell you, "The way it hugs the road—you'll have to experience it for yourself."

You could ask him, "What is your family like?" The visual man might tell you, "They're all tall and dark like me, except my sister, who is short and fair." An auditory man might say, "I can hear the family now. They always shout at each other over dinner." The feelings man may answer, "It's a close, happy family. We stay in touch."

Always be prepared to ask the "Why, What, and How" questions. When you do, be sure that your body language indicates attentiveness (lean forward), and that your words and tone indicate sincere curiosity.

Instead of feeling interrogated, he'll be flattered at your interest in him. He'll think you're a terrific conversationalist; he'll "open up" a little more, and you'll be on your way to learning his Love Language.

For example, if a man tells you he likes to go hang gliding, don't just say, "Oh, that's nice." Or, even if *you've* always wanted to try it, refrain from saying so for the moment; instead, remember the Why, What, and How questions. Say, "What do you like about gliding?"

If he's visual he might tell you he likes the view from above. If he's a hearing type, he may say he likes the silence. If he's a feelings man, he may say he feels free in the air.

If you've asked the Why, What, or How question and he says he doesn't know, be prepared to suggest answers in various Love Languages. For example, you ask him, "What did you like best about living at the beach?" Simple question, but he may not have thought about it. Be prepared for him to say, "Oh, I don't know—it was just nice."

Follow up. If by now you suspect he's visual, suggest to him, "You must have had a wonderful view. How were the sunsets?" If you suspect he's auditory, "There's nothing like the roar of the ocean. How did it sound when it was stormy?" Or if you suspect he's a feelings man, "The ocean has so many moods. How did it feel being so close to it?"

Watch his face and listen closely to his responses. If he says "Uh, it was okay," you probably guessed wrong on his Love Language. No problem. You've now narrowed it down to two possibilities. If, on the other hand, he comes alive at your suggestion and starts talking animatedly, you *may* have guessed right. But don't jump to conclusions from one positive response. Keep checking, trying other questions. You're looking for a pattern.

There's hardly a man alive who doesn't love a woman expressing sincere interest in what he thinks, hanging on his every word. You may feel uneasy asking so many questions, but don't worry. For him, the time will fly by, he'll be enjoying himself—and he'll probably think you're fascinating (although he won't know why). Nevertheless, he may feel embarrassed about "monopolizing" the conversation and say, "Gee, you ask a lot of questions. . . ." Or, "Hey, I've been doing all the talking. . . ."

Act surprised, but be prepared for this with a couple of answers you've rehearsed ahead of time and feel comfortable with. For the ". . . lot of questions," try, "Oh! I guess I have. But you know, you are a *very* interesting man." For the ". . . all the talking," try, "Oh! Have you? I hadn't noticed. The time's just flown by." Remember, if you come back with anything along the lines of, "Well, you're so interesting," I *guarantee* you he'll love it.

By the end of your first date, you will have probably detected enough of a pattern in his answers to give you a handle on his Love Language. As an immediate side benefit of The Love Plan, he will undoubtedly want to see you again—and you will know whether or not you want to.

At this point, if he still meets your Man Plan, you are ready to take the next steps: confirming his Love Language, understanding it more fully, and learning the special magic that will draw him irresistibly to you.

The Visual Man

6

YOUR MAN MAY AT FIRST SEEM INSCRUTABLE, BUT you will be able to look into his soul. Look deeply into his eyes—not just to appear sexy or interested—look because his eyes will truly mirror what he is thinking.

Believe it or not, in almost every civilization, no matter what the language or society, a man's or woman's eye movements will mirror his or her inner thoughts and Love Language. It doesn't matter how old or what the life experience of the person is, eye movements will tell you more than words. No matter what a man's words say, his eyes won't lie.

For example, everyone tends to look up when they're visualizing something. The visualizing man looks up a lot. If you suspect your new man's Love Language is visual, ask him, "What's your apartment like?" He'll probably answer right away—with a *visual* description: "It's got brown carpet and a yellow kitchen." His eyes will probably look up and to one side or the other, an indication that he's remembering something visual.

Keep asking "neutral" questions until you are sure that you are right about his Love Language. Don't "lead" him by asking, "What does your office *look* like?" If you do, he's liable to take the visual clue and respond visually even if he's an auditory or feelings man. Instead, ask, "What is your office like?"

Remember, if he should ask you, "Why all the questions?" you can't go wrong with something like, "Oh, I'm so transparent. You can *see* how interested I am in you. . . ." After all, you really are, aren't you? No man can resist sincere interest and sympatico Love Language.

You may find your visualizer has a definite pattern of looking up to the same side whenever he's visualizing while remembering, and looking up to the opposite side when he's imagining something in the future.

Visual Tests

For example, he may consistently look up and to the right when answering such "past tense" questions as, "What was your family house like?" You will really have a "fix" on him if he is equally consistent about looking up and to the left when answering questions such as, "What would your dream house be like?" If he has this pattern, you will soon be able to tell whether he's visualizing from the past or in the future—even if he doesn't say a word. You will seem to read his mind.

He may not have this right-left pattern. Also, he may not be totally consistent. Some people visualize, especially in their imaginations, by staring straight ahead with a glassy-eyed, fixed stare and dilated pupils. It really doesn't matter. Keep watching, and your visual man's own individual pattern will emerge.

You may notice that the visual man's breathing is often high and shallow and that his shoulders are tense when he's visualizing.

Once you have pinpointed where he looks when he's seeing something in his mind, you will forever be able to tell when he has a visual picture. Then you can find out what it is. How? Simply ask, "What do you see?" Or, "How do you picture that?" Or, "Do you have a clear image?"

For example, you ask, "Would you like steak for dinner?" He doesn't say anything for a few seconds, but he looks up.

If he looks up to his "past" visual side, you'll be fairly sure he's having a visual memory about steak from his past. You might say, "I see you are thinking about a steak you had once before. Or are you remembering another wonderful meal?" If he looks to his future visual side, you might ask, "What kind of dinner do you see us having?"

He'll be so amazed that you can "read his mind"

TYPICAL VISUALIZER

(Remembering something visual from the past)

(Imagining something visual in the future)

YOUR MAN

he'll probably blurt out exactly what he's visualizing.

As soon as you find out what your man's eye movements are when he's visualizing, write it down. Draw a little chart like the one on the previous page, and put it in your Love Plan notebook with your Man Plan.

The Visual Personality

Everyone visualizes to some extent, but true visualizers can't seem to get enough visual stimulation. On the other hand, they can be put off by two much auditory stimulation like loud music or constant chatter.

Visualizers also hate having their feelings spread all over. It is very hard for the visualizing man to express his feelings. You may have to learn to express them for him, or at least help him by giving suggestions and asking questions.

Chances are good you'll run into a visual man. Men are more likely to be highly visual than women in spite of the fact that women are traditionally more interested in fashion and makeup and how they look. The reason is that men find it easier to relate in terms of pictures because they're more concrete, like the engineer who felt he could understand his feelings better if he made charts and drawings of them.

The visual man prefers face-to-face meetings over long phone calls. When he's angry, he's likely to clam up and give you the silent treatment rather than rant and rave. When he drives a car he checks the rearview mirror a lot and watches the other cars and the road carefully.

The visual man is a neat, often stylish dresser. He makes notes of everything. He's organized. His facial expressions are a cue to his emotions. No poker face, he smiles easily and has a discernible frown.

A friend of mine was dating a man who, she complained, "never looks me in the eye." She was worried. "Do you think there's something wrong with him? Maybe he's hiding something from me. Another woman. Six ex-wives. A prison record? I just can't figure it out."

It turned out the man she was dating was just highly visual. His eye movements were very natural for him, just a sign that he was making pictures in his mind while he was talking to her.

Learning this helped my friend understand that her man wasn't *trying* to hide anything from her. She also understood that much of this man was, nevertheless, going to remain hidden from her unless she learned his Love Language. The Love Plan showed her how, and soon their dating blossomed into a real romance.

Men are most happy when they feel understood and communicated with, so use the words he likes and he'll like you. The visualizer's words are always easy to identify. Here is a list of visual words and expressions. Everyone uses them, but visualizers much more so.

If your man seems to go out of his way to express himself visually, if he seems to use these words a lot, you should learn to use them, too. They work like magic on the visual man. The visual clue words are in italics.

What Your Visual Lover Is Likely to Say to You

From my *perspective* our relationship *looks* good.
I *see* what you mean.
Look at that beautiful *view.*
Imagine how it would be.
I have an *image* of my ideal woman.
I like to *observe* human nature.
I enjoy finding new ways of *looking* at things.
Do you get the *picture?*
I have a *clearer* idea now.
It all seems *vague* to me.
I don't like *shiny bright* things.
I prefer *muted* hues.
That fur bedspread sure *looks* good to me.
The more I *look* at you, the *clearer* a *picture* I have of what we're going to do tonight.
Seeing you naked makes me want to *paint* you.
I could *see* a destructive *pattern* with my ex.
I just can't *picture* myself doing that.
That *looks* like a good idea.
My mind is a *blank.*
Looking back at my past relationships, I can begin to *see the light.*

What You Should Say Back

I really *see* what you mean.
I can *visualize* that.
How do you *see* our relationship?

I can *imagine* us having a good time doing that.
I can *picture* us making love right now.
You sure *look* good in that shirt.
Those *colors* make you *look* really healthy.
That *shine* in your *eyes* turns me on.
I could *see* us getting older together.
We need a *clearer image* of the problem.
Let me try to *cast some light* on the subject.
Let's get some *enlightenment* this weekend.
That was a *colorful* example you gave.
Let's go to the country and *look* at some local *color.*
I'd love to take *pictures* of you.

Visual Expressions

You may be thinking, "For sure, if I start talking like that he's going to be suspicious and begin to wonder what I'm up to."

Just the opposite. The visual way you will be expressing yourself will sound *natural* to him. He'll be delighted that he's found someone with whom he can really communicate. He'll never catch on if you don't tell him.

If you feel nervous about talking totally visually, try a little at first. You'll see how quickly you gain the visual man's attention.

While the constant use of visual words may seem artificial to you, remember that these are valid, clear, common words. Your thoughts can be expressed just as honestly with them as with other words. The effort you make in learning to communicate visually is a growth and learning experience for you, as well as the sure path to getting your man. So practice it faithfully.

Soon you'll be using only visual expressions with him; it will come naturally to you. Then you'll see that, no matter how outrageously you "mirror" his visual love language and thinking, he'll only be more sure you really understand him.

And you know what? You really will!

More Visual Clues

How the Visual Lover Will Spend His Time

Photography
Art collecting
Coin or stamp collecting
Going to the movies
Watching television
Taking the picturesque route
Windowshopping
Reading
Buying clothes
Decorating his house
Primping
Landscaping
Collecting antiques
Collecting classic cars

What the Visualizer Does for a Living

Filmmaker
Cameraman
Photographer

Decorator
Clothes designer
Artist
Signpainter
Housepainter
Hair dresser
Makeup artist
Architect
Landscape design
Graphic arts
Advertising
Publishing
Computer graphics
Airplane pilot
Race car designer

How to Make Love to the Visual Man

Your visual man will talk about how things look most of the time. His beautifully arranged home and exquisite designer's wardrobe will give him away. You should also be perfect in every visual detail for him.

Dress so that you are always pretty as a picture. If you're the type to bop out of bed and put makeup on in the morning, this is the man to do it for. He'll love you in far-out fashions, as long as they're not any further out than he is.

You can tell what he likes to see by looking at his surroundings. His favorite color, his favorite fabric, his favorite pictures. Dress in his favorite color. Dress like he does. If he's preppy, you dress preppy. If he's elegant, you be elegant.

Tell him, "You're gorgeous when you're naked." Or, "Look at the way my nipples pucker up for you." Always plan your outings to include memorable views. Pick restaurants by the ocean, pick a table that looks out over the boats. Park on a view spot and look at the city lights, enjoy the mountains. Give him a picture book. Take lots of photos and give him some.

Wear sexy clothes—garter belts, or tight jeans. Always make love with the lights on or you'll kill half the effect for this man.

Set up your bedroom to be visually exciting. Leave erotic magazines around with lots of pictures. Explore his fantasies by asking him to erotic movies or going through picture books with him.

The visual lover wants to stop and look before he does anything. Don't rush up and hug him or try to get physically too close too soon. He wants a good look at the total picture before he gets into a feeling mood.

Never ramble on about your feelings to a visual man, at least not in the beginning of the relationship. In a later chapter you'll learn to get him to "see" your feelings. But keep your deepest feelings to yourself until you've read through Chapter Seventeen, "Casting a Spell." By then you'll have a better idea of how to get him in touch with his feelings.

If you start telling a visual man about your feelings in the beginning, you won't get much response. It's likely that he'll feel uncomfortable. He may even want to leave.

As most people now understand, women tend to be more into feelings than men. Some women actually feel that a man is "wrong" by not communicating on a feelings level. A few even go so far as to righteously insist that the man "open up" and relate on a feelings level. This is the worst mistake a woman could make.

Communicate your feelings to the visual man gradually, in visual terms. He'll "get the picture" instantly, and it will undoubtedly "brighten" his "outlook" to know you enjoy "seeing" him. Remember, visual men *have* feelings; they just find it hard to express them with "feeling" words.

Later, after deep communication has been established (in his "language"), you may want to explain a little about different Love Languages to your lover. At that point, he won't be threatened, and because he loves you, he will be curious to find out *your* Love Language too.

If you follow The Love Plan, you will learn to speak any man's Love Language, and you will be able to make any man love you.

In the meantime, if you're with a visual man, *think pictures.*

What You Are

If you are visual, you may be known for your good fashion sense, or your innate ideas about new and exciting decor. You always look well put together. You have experimented extensively with makeup and colors and you never go out without looking good. You invest a lot in your wardrobe. You have a manicure regularly and wouldn't be caught dead with chipped polish. Your house is neat and organized.

You won't have any trouble relating to the visual

man. You will always look your best and he will appreciate it.

If you are auditory, you probably aren't known for your sartorial elegance or your delightful decor. Instead, you are the one people turn to when they need to talk because you are a very good listener. You are the intellectual of your crowd, the lay therapist for all your friends.

You will have to make a special effort to relate to the visual man, to see and think in pictures, and to make yourself and your surroundings visually appealing to him. Make sure he sees what you're talking about. Don't just tell him, describe things and events in visual terms.

If you are into your feelings, you are casual about fashion and intellectual pursuits. You are more likely to be a comfort to friends, a soft touch for everyone, and well-loved by all. There has probably never been a stray who came to your door and was turned away. You have a terrifically accurate sense of intuition and probably know what other people are feeling before they do.

When relating to the visual man, it will be important for you to hold your feelings in check. Don't cry all over him or spill out your every childhood trauma. Let him *see* what a sensitive person you are. *Show* him how much fun you can be. Take extra care with your appearance.

The Auditory Man

7

YOUR AUDITORY LOVER IS A MAN WHO IS INTO sounds. There's nothing wrong with his eyes, and his feelings are normal. He just relates better to music than pictures, is more in tune with the inner logic of words than with feelings.

This auditory man could be hard to reach at first because his auditory preference might lead him to long conversations in his head with himself or his alter ego. If you don't understand how to get into his conversations, you will feel left out.

Auditory Eyes

To confirm that your man is auditory, and to gain access to his "inner voices," watch his eyes closely, because once again, his eyes are the mirror of his soul. A man who is primarily a hearer can of course visualize as well, so don't be dismayed if he looks up once in a while, but the hearer looks mostly to the side. Watch his eyes glance to the right or to the left, as if he were looking toward his ears.

It's important not to mix up an auditory and a visual man. One woman who was dating an auditory man didn't understand how to talk to him. She told me this story of an almost-disastrous date.

"I took him out on a surprise Sunday afternoon date. I thought we'd drive to the desert and see the wild flowers. It was spring. There's nothing more beautiful than the purples and yellows and bright reds of desert wild flowers.

"I said to him, 'Look at the view over there,' and he practically yawned in my face. Finally, we got to a viewpoint where I'd arranged to surprise him with a picnic. But he wasn't hungry. He was disappointed the whole day because the radio in my car wasn't working. He wondered how we could get through lunch without music.

"I had a new hair style and a new outfit, neither of which he noticed. I think he's unconscious."

A week or so later, I had an opportunity to meet this man at a social function. He was so obviously auditory. He really liked the woman who'd taken him out for a visual day on the desert, but in confidence he told me, "She never seems to be really listening to me. She doesn't seem to hear what I say to her." It didn't take long before this woman learned to relate to her man on an auditory level.

Auditory Tests

To test your man's auditory response, ask him questions like, "What's your favorite music?" Watch him look to the left or right (in a few cases, it can be down and to one side), showing you his pattern for hearing things in his mind.

Should he not have any favorite music, or hardly ever listen, or seem uncomfortable with "sound" questions, or show upward or straight-down eye response, those are all immediate clues that your man is not primarily auditory.

Ever notice how he loves the sound of a motor running, or can hear the least little ticking sound in the house. Wonder how he can tell the difference between a Maserati and a Ferrari just by hearing them? Does he have music on all the time? He may be very auditory.

To further confirm that you have a "hearer," ask him simple but telling questions like, "What do you remember about your childhood?" Should he tell you, "I lived near a railroad track and I remember the sound of the trains going by all the time," he is auditory. While he's telling you this you'll notice his sideways eye movements.

A visual man could have easily and just as rightly answered, "I was raised in a neat neighborhood with green lawns in front of all the houses. Our house was red brick and had two gables that stuck out on the second floor." A feelings man might have said, "I had a really happy childhood."

You ask him about his family. The auditory man tells you he has two sisters and he loves them except for their nasal voices, which make him avoid talking to them. He says he doesn't visit them much either

TYPICAL AUDITORY MAN

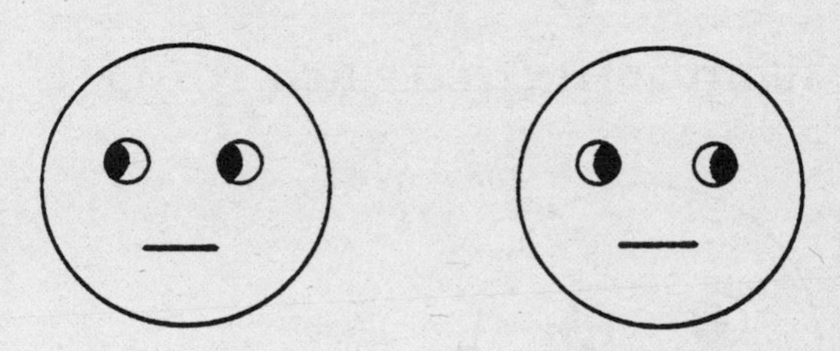

YOUR MAN

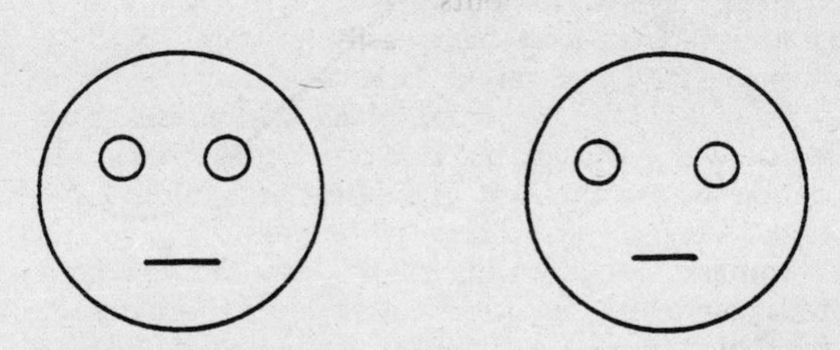

AUDITORY MAN (TELEPHONE POSTURE)

because their kids are really noisy. The visual man, on the other hand, tells you what his family looks like, and the feelings man tells you how much he misses them.

If you ask the auditory man what he liked most about his ex-wife, you might be surprised to find he liked the sound of her voice, or the way she always listened to him.

Each time he answers one of your questions, notice your hearing man's eye movements. As soon as you detect a pattern, make note of it, or a little drawing similar to the one on page 64.

There is one other sign of an auditory person doing his thing—the telephone posture. He sits with his hand on the side of his head as if he's talking on the telephone. During this time, you can be almost positive he's having an internal conversation with himself. See the drawing on page 65.

The Auditory Personality

The auditory man will prefer in-person or telephone conversation to writing letters or memos. He spends a lot of time on the telephone. As soon as he gets in the car, he turns the radio on. When he comes into his house, he turns on the stereo. He loves the sounds of voices.

He is quick to let you hear about it if he's angry about something. He is articulate and expresses himself well. He enjoys debating almost any issue. He is knowledgeable and enjoys telling people what he knows.

He is a sensible, but not fancy, dresser. He often

plays a musical instrument for relaxation. He loves concerts and other listening experiences.

The auditory man is also likely to have conversations with himself in his head while he's talking with you. The best way to find out about these conversations is to watch his eyes.

For example, you ask him, "What movie would you most like to see?" He doesn't answer right away. As a matter of fact, you're not even sure he heard you. You notice, though, that his eyes are directly off to one side. He did hear you, and he's discussing some possible answers in his head. But he won't necessarily tell you what they are; he may just say, "I don't know."

However, as a careful observer, you know that this man has just had an auditory experience, all by himself. So how do you find out what he's thinking about? Ask him. Don't forget the Why, How, and What questions. Give him choices in his Love Language.

Most auditory men are internally oriented. It may take lots of loving, artful questions to find out about the conversations he has in his head, but once you do, he'll feel so understood, he'll never want to leave you. You'll be the first and only woman to ever know his inner thoughts.

Begin by asking him if he'd prefer staying home and listening to music or just sitting around and talking instead of going out to a movie. Give him some auditory alternative to the proposed visual experience.

Judy, a twenty-six-year-old teacher, was dating a man who was pulling away. She was madly in love with him, but couldn't figure out how to reach him.

As a teacher for retarded children, she had learned to communicate by touch a lot. Children would feel her love and be calmed. She tried the same technique on the man she was in love with, but unfortunately, he didn't respond at all to her affection.

She was also concerned because he always seemed to look away from her. "He has a slightly furtive look about him," she told me. After studying his eye movements and asking him a few test questions, she found out he was definitely into sounds.

In order to reach him, she began to talk first, before touching. She told him stories about the children she worked with, stories about her family, her friends. "He couldn't get enough of my talking to him," she reported.

Next, while she continued to talk to him in the way he liked best, she began to slowly touch his arm, then his chest, then the back of his neck, his lips and eyes. At last he was reacting to her affection and actually touching her back. They are still together.

You can tell if your man is auditory by using all your own senses. Watch his eyes. Listen to the words he uses. Test his responses to pictures, to sounds, to feelings. The auditory man always responds best to sounds, even the sound of his own voice.

The man who is primarily into experiencing the world through sounds will also use lots of words that relate to how things sound. If you're not sure about his eye movements, listen to what he says. The hearing man's words give him away too. (The auditory clue words are italicized.)

What Your Auditory Lover Is Likely To Say to You

It *sounds like* fun.
Let's *talk* things over.
Do you *hear* what I'm saying?
Tell me what you think.
I can *tune in* or *tune out* when I want.
The *tone* of someone's *voice* is important.
I don't like a lot of *raucous noise* at home.
Listen to what I'm *saying.*
Do you hear the *rhythm?*
Harmony is important to me.
It's *clear as a bell* to me now.
I'll be a *sounding* board for you.
My ex gave me a lot of *static.*
That has a negative *ring* to it.

What You Should Say Back

I love the *sound* of your *voice.*
I *hear* what you're *saying.*
Listen to this *music.*
You and I could *make beautiful music* together.
Your idea really *clicks* with me.
When we kiss, I *hear bells ringing.*
I feel like we're *in perfect harmony* when we're together.
What you just *said rings a bell* with me.
Your idea *sounds good* to me.
I can *hear* that you want to *listen* to the *stereo* tonight.

That *sounds* right to me.
I feel *tuned in to your frequency.*
Ask yourself what's right and *listen* carefully to the answer.
Something *tells* me we're right for each other.
I have this idea about us *rattling around* in my head.

More Auditory Clues

How the Auditory Lover Will Spend His Time

Listening to music
Going to concerts
Talking on the telephone
Playing a musical instrument
Dancing at a disco
Hearing a lecture
Listening to the radio
With the television on, but not necessarily watching
Constructing conversations in his head
Eavesdropping on other people's conversations
Operating a C.B. radio

What the Auditory Lover Does for a Living

Sound engineer
Stereo salesman
Stereo repairman
Piano tuner
Telephone sales

Teacher
Radio announcer
Therapist
Singer
Musician
Lawyer

How to Make Love to the Auditory Man

Your auditory lover will be more concerned with how things sound than with how they look. That means if he's coming over to spend the night, set up a stack of records on the stereo and turn the music on before you worry about cleaning up your place.

He will always have the very best stereo equipment he can afford and good sound is important to him. Don't worry so much about what you wear. Worry more about how you sound. Is your voice shrill or too high? Listen to yourself on a tape recorder. If you don't think you sound good, practice lowering and mellowing out your voice before he gets there.

Never, ever shriek at him. No matter how angry you are, try to keep your tones well modulated. One thing that will drive this man away almost instantly is a screaming woman.

Don't change the music at his house or in his car unless you're absolutely sure it's okay. Try to match your tone to his in every way. For example, if he plays classical, you play classical. If he speaks in a soft quiet voice, you should too. If he talks slowly, you speak slowly.

Talk to him about the sounds of love. Tell him, "Your voice turns me on." Pant gently in his ear.

Talk to him while you're making love. Tell him, "That's a perfect rhythm for me." Or, "It's amazing how our bodies seem to be in tune with each other."

"Listen to me, please," this man seems to be saying. So listen and give him the sounds that say you're listening. Don't just sit there and look into his eyes; say things like, "Yes, I hear you."

Your auditory man will love things like birds singing, the rustle of leaves, special love songs, wind chimes. He'll be turned off by kids crying, water dripping, a scratchy stereo, and loud noises or shouting.

With your auditory lover, express yourself. I remember George, a studio sound engineer I dated. He never seemed happy with our lovemaking unless I let him know in a verbal way that I appreciated what he did. "That's just right," I'd have to assure him. He just loved to hear, "I'm coming, I'm coming," at the moment of orgasm, and other sounds of lovemaking were really important to him as well.

I did an experiment with George and found that if I just came quietly without making any sounds he took longer than usual to have his own orgasm. But if I screamed and made lots of noise, George came almost instantly. I was always torn when we made love. Part of me wanted to make him happy, part of me wanted him to keep going.

If you have an auditory lover, the key is to talk a lot as well as listen. I used to read erotic poetry out loud in bed to George, and we even sang together. Practice a running dialogue for lovemaking.

Learn to say things like, "The sound of your voice turns me on." Or, "I hear what you're saying." And,

"That sounds wonderful." The auditory man needs constant verbal reassurance of your love and attention, even when you're making love.

Looking deeply into the hearing man's eyes won't make him believe you really hear him, nor will a reassuring hug make him feel understood. You must talk to him.

Say his name often and in a certain loving tone of voice. Men who are into sounds love the sound of their own name. When he talks to you, show you are listening in an auditory way. Speak up every once in a while, it's important to your auditory man. If you have an auditory man, think sounds.

What You Are

If you are auditory, you will be in sync with your auditory man. You will hear each other loud and clear. Enjoy long hours talking to him on the phone, discussing philosophy or the universe. You have met your match.

If you are a visual person, you might become frustrated by your auditory lover's lack of interest in your beautiful new dress, or the new way you're wearing your hair. Don't be upset. He's more interested in the inner you; he appreciates that you look good but it's not the most important thing in his life. At last, here's a man who will really listen to what you have to say. Talk to him.

If you are a feelings woman, be sure to talk to the auditory man while you're touching him. Don't just assume that he understands your feelings because you have them. Tell him how you feel. Let him know you're listening to him.

The Feelings Man

8

THE FEELINGS MAN WEARS HIS HEART ON HIS sleeve. He is perhaps the man you will find yourself most sympatico with because he is so much like you.

Traditionally, women have been taught to show their feelings more than men. Women have learned to react from their feelings. So this man may be the easiest of all to establish rapport and intimacy with right away.

Feeling Eyes

To discover whether your man perceives his world mostly through his feelings, once again, you must watch his eyes. If he looks down a lot, he's probably into feelings. When his eyes are down, he may be recalling a feeling from his past and living it all over again. Or he may be feeling something that is new and having to do with the moment.

Test for Feelings

You'll want to confirm your man's eye clues with other tests, since a feelings man may look downward and to one side or the other, just as some auditory men do. To test your man to find out how feelings oriented he really is, ask such questions as, "What was your childhood like?"

The feelings man will probably answer, "I had a happy (or unhappy) childhood." Emphasize and follow up. "That's wonderful. Tell me about it." Or, "How awful. What made it so unhappy?" Soon you'll have a wealth of information about him and his family, and he'll feel really understood.

He won't tell you what his childhood home looked like, or the sounds of his childhood. He'll tell you how his childhood felt.

You may want to ask this man, "What's your favorite way of relaxing?" He would most likely breathe deeply and answer you in feelings instead of sights or sounds. For example, the feelings man might tell you, "I like to soak in a real hot jacuzzi. I like to feel the bubbles." Or he may tell you, "I love to have a massage."

When he's telling you, you'll notice his eyes go down and to one side. That's his feeling side. Once you have figured out where he looks when he's feeling something, this is the easiest man to get close to. All you have to do is ask, "How do you feel?" and chances are, he'll tell you either with his words or his body language or both.

When you have pinpointed the direction in which your man looks when he's remembering or having a feeling, you should draw a little chart. See the drawing on page 124.

Your feelings man will make his decisions based on whether they feel good. For him to be in love, the relationship has to *feel* right. He will wait for his feelings to tell him it's love, and you can't rush him. The good part is that once he feels that you're the woman for him, nobody can change his mind.

After you have pinpointed the feelings man, you can always find out what's going on in his mind. Ask him, "How do you feel about our relationship?" or "How do you feel about going to the movies tonight?"

You can identify this man by his eye movements and by the words he uses. Listen closely to what he says. His words are easy to identify. (The feelings clue words are italicized.)

What Your Feelings Lover Is Likely to Say to You

I don't *feel* right about going out tonight.
Do you *understand* what I mean?
I like to *keep in touch* with my friends.
I *hate* to *hurt* anyone.
Do you *feel* the wind blowing?
My ideal woman is *warm* and *exciting.*
Bonding is important to me.
Let's *get a grasp* on ourselves.
I prefer *warm, close* friendships.
I try to *keep abreast* of my family.

TYPICAL FEELINGS MAN **YOUR MAN**

I'm *sensitive* about that.
That *shook me up.*
I can't seem to *get a handle* on this
That left a *sour taste in my mouth.*
My ex was *cold* and *unresponsive.*
I like to *reach out* to friends during *hard* times.
I don't *feel comfortable* in a little car.

What You Should Say Back

I can *understand* how you *feel.*
I can *empathize* with you.
That's a *heavy* problem.
How do you *feel* about our relationship?
Let's stay *in touch.*
That story really *moves* me.
Let's *walk through* the problem.
I *sense* that you're a *warm* person.
I love the way your body *feels.*
Touch is very important to me.
I *love* you to *hold me tightly.*
I have good *feelings* about us.

The Feelings Personality

The feelings man is often an athletic type. He has a solid muscular body and is likely to dress comfortably rather than fashionably. He likes to talk while he's doing something physical like jogging. When he's angry, he's liable to storm out of a room or pound a table.

It's hard for the feelings man to sit still through long meetings and discussions. He is quick to kiss or hug or express his emotions physically.

Of all men, the feelings lover is the most sensitive. He will be the first to get hurt in a relationship. He will also be the first to love. It's important not to approach this man either visually or auditorily, because he won't be moved.

Elizabeth, a secretary in her late twenties, was dating a feelings man for some time without knowing it. They had constant problems. He felt unappreciated and she felt he wasn't listening to her.

"I talk to him and talk to him and yet I never seem to get through," she told me. "He tells me he doesn't feel understood. I know he doesn't think I care about him, but I do. How can I convince him?"

I asked Elizabeth to describe her usual date with Henry. It went something like this.

"I rush home from work and spend two hours getting fixed up to go out with him. I straighten the house. I clean the kitchen. I do my hair and fix my makeup and put on my best-looking clothes. Then I put music on the stereo.

"By the time he comes to pick me up, I'm perfect. But he hardly notices. I can be all dressed up and he shows up in Levis.

"The first thing he does is grab me and mess up

my hair and makeup, practically before we've been together five minutes.

"We go to a movie and then out to eat and then home to my place or his. Usually, he only spends the night on weekends. During the week, we sleep apart."

Part of Elizabeth's problem was that she was doing sight and sound activities, like going to movies and putting on the stereo, with a feelings man. She had to learn to do different things.

Instead of talking to him all the time, or spending her time fixing her apartment and her hair, she began to concentrate on how he felt. She had a cold drink ready for him and hor d'oeuvres or a hot bath or a quick backrub. She began to touch him as she spoke, accompanying all her sounds with touch.

They are still together and happily involved because Elizabeth learned to change from her usual sight and sound way of operating into George's feelings system.

I'll never forget Michael, my feelings lover. We had the same Love Language to start with—we were both into feelings, so it was easy to fall in love. I felt so loved by him because he was always being physically affectionate. There wasn't a moment when he wasn't petting, kissing, touching, or caressing me. We cried together and we laughed easily.

In bed, Michael loved satin sheets, warm lotions and oils rubbed on his body, and lots of feathers and vibrators. He loved it when I talked about how smooth, hard, or sexy he felt to me. "That feels fantastic," I was always sure to tell him. My emotions were like food for him. He wanted to understand how I felt and to express his own feelings on every subject.

Michael's life was designed to feel good rather than to look good. He appreciated good food, fur bedspreads and comfortable clothing. "I understand how you feel" were the words he most yearned to hear. Together we enjoyed wallowing in our senses and experimenting with new ways of making love.

More Feeling Clues

How the Feelings Lover Will Spend His Time

Lying in the sun
Swimming
Dancing
Working out
Eating
Running
Cooking
Drinking
Smoking
Getting high
Sailing
Participating in sports

What the Feelings Lover Does for a Living

Cook
Masseur or physical therapist
Sculpture

Hairdresser
Psychologist
Counselor
Teacher
Minister
Carpenter
Construction worker
Doctor
Dentist

How to Make Love to the Feelings Man

Your feelings lover will be more concerned with how things feel than how they look or sound. Wear your soft velvets, cashmeres and smooth silks for him. Make up the bed with satin sheets. Forget about your knobby knits, and most of all, be comfortable, because then you'll be on his wavelength.

Always touch your feeling lover when you're together. If you can, touch him in a sensitive place, like the back of his neck, while you're saying his name. That way you're always sure to get his attention.

Lots of hugs and kisses and tender caresses will make him respond with plenty of love toward you. Don't be shy. Throw your arms around him, rub up against him. Tell him often how he feels to you.

Say things to him like, "You feel so smooth on the inside of your thigh, I just love to touch you there." Or, "I love the feel of your warm lips." Or, "That sweater feels so good. Let me touch it."

The feelings man is also certain to be more into his other senses like taste and smell. Be sure to appeal to those as well. Find out his favorite perfume, and then wear it. Give him your favorite scent to wear. Feed him grapes with your fingers.

Get carried away with your senses in the bedroom. Try chocolate poured on you that he licks off. There is nothing this man likes better than being touched. Rub him all over with baby oil and he'll purr like a kitten.

Experiment with him. He'll love whatever you want to do, as long as it feels good.

The way to talk to your feelings man is while you're touching him. That way, you know he'll listen and probably react favorably to what you're saying.

The man who's into feelings is sensitive and hurts easily, but he'll be sensitive to your feelings as well as his own.

Once you have established a loving atmosphere by putting your loved one at ease in his own feelings language you can explore his receptiveness to sights and sounds. But the original good feelings spring from communicating in a mutually understood Love Language. So start by getting on his wavelength, then add your own.

What You Are

If you are a feelings woman, you are in luck if you find a man who matches you. Most men are visual or auditory, but some feelings men do exist. If you find one, you will finally have a man who is as sensitive as you are. He will share your joys and pains. You are an easy match.

If you are a visual woman, you will have to make a special effort to reach the feelings man. He will be more interested in how you feel than how you look. He will appreciate soft touches and caresses and a bubble bath more than a movie or a fashion show.

If you are an auditory woman, you can reach the feelings man by talking to him about your feelings. At the same time, be sure to touch him. Be sure to ask him how he feels about things before you blurt out something he hates.

Secret Reflections

9

HAVE YOU EVER NOTICED HOW LOVERS SEEM TO look alike? How they often wear the same style of clothes, even the same colors and shades?

Look closely at people in love. You'll notice that they tend to look alike, dress alike, and even sit in exactly the same posture. Watch how they'll cross or uncross a leg at almost the same time. Notice how both of them will cross their arms, or how they'll both stand with their weight on the same foot.

The reason lovers are so similar is that they are so "in tune" with each other they act alike without even thinking about it consciously. Sometimes, just by observing how deliciously alike a couple has suddenly become, you can tell people are in love before they even know it themselves.

Being "In Tune"

Even in nonromantic situations, notice how men automatically seem to like other men and women who are like themselves? You may have noticed how alike your own friends are in areas of education, background, jobs, and families. It's inevitable.

If you're a writer like me, you'll have a lot of friends in the publishing business. If you're a nurse, you'll be more likely to know people in medicine.

If you're a college graduate, most of your friends will be too. If you play tennis, so will a lot of your friends. And it's not just a matter of finding mutual things to talk about.

Men and women both tend to like and trust the familiar. The most familiar is themselves, which is why people tend to find others who have taste and values similar to their own.

When you find a man you want to be in love with you, look for the similarities. If you can emphasize the ways in which you are alike, he will automatically trust you and begin to feel close to you.

Many women feel, "If a man sees the real me, if he discovers my pure true wonderful inner person, then he will fall in love with me." That may be, but in order to show him the "real" you, you have to first be able to get close to him and communicate with him in a way he can understand. Otherwise, he may never be open to your special charms.

To get close to the man you want, The Love Plan calls for you to make yourself appear to be as much like him as possible. In Chapters Six, Seven and Eight, you learned to talk to him in his special Love Language. Now we add another dimension—physical mirroring.

Physical Mirroring

Physical mirroring is one of the most powerful getting-close techniques that anybody can learn to do instantly with no training. Physical mirroring will get you closer to a man, even if it's the only Love Plan technique you use. You can start practicing immediately without waiting for Mr. Right. Then when you find him, he'll find you irresistible.

What is physical mirroring? It is the technique of being "in sync" with a man—subtly matching his appearance, posture and movements.

Think of it this way: If the way you look and act is at odds with the way a man looks and acts, the message he unconsciously receives is that you disagree with how he looks and acts. Nobody likes to be disagreed with. On the other hand, if you always seem to match how he looks and acts, you are *validating* him; he will feel he can trust you and will want to be with you.

In a nonobvious manner, casually sit like he sits and stand like he stands. If he crosses his legs, you cross your legs. If he leans forward, you lean forward. If he puts his hand on his knee, you put your hand on your knee. But don't cross your hands in front of you unless he does.

Crossing in front has been known as "don't-get-near-me" body language, but if the man you want does it, you do it. Then, when you're "in sync" with his rhythms totally, you can get him to uncross his arms.

You may not believe that a person's physical posture is very important, but studies have shown that you can tell a lot more by studying a man's or woman's body language than by listening to the words he or she says.

Body language in general has been found to have more weight than anything else. In other words, if a man tells you he loves you and his facial expression and body language say he doesn't, you're safer believing the body language.

For example, you've just gone on your first date with a man you like. He says he really had a good time and he'll call you soon. You notice his arms are crossed in front of him and he isn't making much eye contact with you. You can probably forget about hearing from him.

Remember that a man has a lot more conscious control over what he's saying than he does over his body language. When a man's words and body language contradict each other, his body language is revealing how he really feels. Body language is the true reflection of the inner man. For true love to develop, you must be in touch with the inner man. That's why it's so important for you to learn and practice physical mirroring.

Physical mirroring is almost as important as the "mirroring" of a man's Love Language. This physical mirroring technique may at first sound so mechanical that you're sure he'll suspect something if you do it. But if you're subtle with your movements, not abrupt or inappropriate, he'll never know.

Unbeknownst to you, people have probably mirrored your own actions. Don't you remember the last time you bought more clothes than you should have from a persuasive saleswoman? Didn't she seem to be "in tune" with you in a way?

She was probably mirroring you, your voice, your

tone, your rhythm. The most successful salespeople automatically mirror their customers. The customers like and trust the salesperson, and therefore buy more easily than they might otherwise.

Of course you should never mirror someone's physical disability. For example, if a man has a facial tic, don't you start twitching too. But if he sits with his chin in his hand, or with his arms crossed, or leaning backward or forward, or with his arms open on the back of the chair, or any variation of *normal* body postures, you should try to mirror him.

I have been mirroring people for several years now and so have thousands of others in their daily work. I have mirrored judges while testifying as an expert witness on relationships, I have mirrored potential employers while applying for jobs, and I have mirrored many, many men. I have always found that mirroring was successful in establishing instant trust and rapport.

Didn't any of them ever *suspect?* Not really. They may have *noticed,* but that's very different. An interesting thing happens when a man notices that you are matching his posture or movements. It seems to him that he is leading you, and you are following him without being aware of it. What does he conclude? That *you* are strongly affected by *him.* For a man, there is no stronger allure.

Clearly, for this technique to work properly, it must be done in a subtle, nonmechanical way. This is not the kid's game of "Monkey See, Monkey Do." Your mirroring needn't be precise and shouldn't be quick. After he shifts position, allow a few seconds to pass, then drift into a similar or matching posture as though you were unconsciously *drawn* into it.

Any woman can easily learn effective mirroring. You don't have to be an Oscar-winning actress. You needn't be apprehensive about trying it. First of all, you *are* sincerely interested in this man or you wouldn't be using The Love Plan with him. There is really nothing devious or wrong about trying to get "in sync" with someone you care about. And remember, even if he notices, the worst that will happen is that his male ego will tell him you're influenced by his powerful personality. So try it!

Practice mirroring on your friends until you are able to change body postures smoothly and unselfconsciously. If you have small children, they are always delighted to be mirrored and you may find new ways to reach and communicate with them too.

You'll quickly see how easy it is. Then try it on a man you'd like to meet, at a gathering or party. Watch what he does. Let's say he's sitting in a chair, holding his drink in his left hand, with one leg crossed over the other. You sit, cross your leg and hold your drink similarly. If he's got a friendly, open attitude, you assume the same. If he leans back, puts one arm over the back of the chair and looks bored, you lean back a little, put your arm over the side of your chair and look bored too.

If he notices anyone, he'll probably notice you. He won't know why, but he'll have a feeling that you might be someone he'd like to meet.

Janet, an attractive but not beautiful, twenty-seven-year-old, never-married, legal secretary, learned to use mirroring to get the upper hand in a competitive situation. She told me about her problem of going out to a club or bar with her women friends and never being able to go home with a guy because her friends always got the good ones.

"I'll be sitting there as if I didn't exist," she told me. "I've tried everything. I've dressed sexier. I laugh loudly at the least little joke and I smile until my mouth feels like it's going to fall off.

"The men ignore me. What makes it worse is that other women sitting right at the same table, sometimes right next to me, are the center of attention. The guys can't take their eyes off them.

"I know I'm not the most beautiful, but I'm not the ugliest either. I have a good figure and I'm a lot of fun, but nobody seems to notice me."

Janet was thinking about plastic surgery, but instead she tried mirroring. The next time she went out with the girls, she stopped trying to attract attention in the ways she used to—by laughing loudly or interrupting. Instead she sat quietly and simply mirrored the man she was interested in. Soon he was giving her all his attention and she never had to go home alone again—unless she wanted to.

By learning these ways of mirroring a man, both physically and in his Love Language, you can also graduate from being a helpless "waiting to be chosen," woman, to a powerful woman in control of your life. You'll never again have to sit at a party or a bar simply passing the time until someone decides to make a move. Now you can make the moves and he'll never know it.

It's true that most men like to feel as if they're doing the pursuing. That's why mirroring is so effective. It allows you to choose a man, make the first moves, and still let him be the aggressor. He'll think he's doing the chasing.

What Shall I Wear?

Another part of physical mirroring has to do with the way you dress. Once you have decided on a man to make your own, you should begin to dress like he does.

With the emphasis on subtle, wear something that will not "fight" what he wears. If he's into denim, don't wear a satin dress. If he's tweedie, don't dress mod. If possible, wear a female version of what he wears.

I remember when I first started dating my husband. He was a popular bachelor with lots of other women interested in him. Two of them were really in love with him.

He invited me to a party at his house and I knew at least one of the other women he was seeing would be there. I wanted to make the right impression.

Instead of trying to figure out what I had to wear that he'd never seen before, or what would make the other women sit up and take notice, or what I had that was the sexiest, I simply figured out what he would wear. Then I wore the same thing.

My rivals both showed up in their finest and sexiest. One wore a Halston. The other wore a very seductive gypsy outfit with her bare midriff beckoning and her cleavage calling. Instead of trying to compete, I wore a simple silk blouse, leather belt, boots and jeans, exactly what my future husband wore that night.

Naturally, he loved my outfit and I got all his attention. He thought I was most appropriately dressed—because I wore *exactly* what he wore. And he never knew I was mirroring him that night until he read this chapter.

Once you forget about yourself and start thinking about the man you want to fall in love with you, you will discover lots of ways to mirror him. Maybe if you're undecided about what to order when you're out to dinner, you could order something similar to what he gets. Perhaps if you're wondering what brand of soap or toothpaste to buy, you could choose his. Little things add up in the mirroring department.

Because women have had to learn more subtle ways of gaining power than men have, women are more flexible. It's always easier for a woman to switch to a man's behavior than for him to switch to hers.

Because you are a woman, you will be able to use these techniques more easily and more gracefully than a man would. Men are certainly less likely, for example, to think of changing outfits to match someone. And the man's reaction to mirroring with clothes? If he notices it at all, he'll think you showed the good taste to learn from him.

One of the women I interviewed who freely admitted she could make any man fall in love with her told me, "I'm like a chameleon. I change according to what the man wants, but I'm still myself. I never lie to them, but I do notice what men want.

"For instance, if a man wants a childlike woman, I'll let the child part of me out when we're together. If he wants a sophisticated woman, I'll let the more sophisticated part of me out. If he wants to laugh and have fun, I do that too. I've never wanted a man to fall in love with me and had him get away."

What she was really doing was unconsciously mirroring just a small part of the men she met. You can mirror his soul, and that's much more powerful. Mirroring is a way to emphasize the similarities between you and the man you love. When a man identifies with you, he is more likely to agree to things, he is easier to convince, and he is more likely to fall in love.

This doesn't mean that you will change who you are. That's impossible and you'd be found out eventually. But you can broaden the way you communicate and the way you reach out. If you're primarily a feelings person, for example, it will actually be a growth experience for you to learn to communicate on visual and auditory wavelengths. You will gain insights, become more adaptable, and have more personal power in more situations than you ever had before.

Some women will always feel that they wouldn't change a thing for a man. "Either he takes me just the way I am, or he can leave," they say. Often, the man chooses to leave.

Barbara, a thirty-five-year-old bachelor, refused to change her bachelor behavior no matter what. She lived in a furnished apartment without a picture on the wall, without curtains, plants, or pets. She was waiting for Mr. Right to come along and rescue her, but in the meantime, she refused to do certain things other women did to attract a man.

"I don't believe in pretending to be something I'm not," she affirmed time and time again. She is also a confirmed bachelor to this day.

Changing the way you are sitting or the way you communicate (from visual to auditory, for example) should not threaten your sense of self, and it's certainly not a step on the way to becoming a subservient woman. To the contrary, it makes you a more adaptable and powerful person. It's fun to learn, people will like you more—and it certainly will help make a man fall in love with you.

More Secret Reflections

10

WE HAVE ALL HEARD OF THE MAN WHO WALKS TO the beat of his own drum. Actually every man has his own rhythm, some more obvious than others. If you think about it, you probably have your own rhythm too.

Mirroring Rhythms

Some people talk fast. Some talk slowly. If you're interested in a fast-talking man, talk faster yourself. If he's slow, you slow down too. That's the simplest form of mirroring a man's rhythm.

Next start observing his less conscious rhythms. Does he tap his fingers? Does he jiggle his foot? If he does, you should unobtrusively and subtly pick up on his motion.

Rhythm mirroring is more subtle than physical mirroring. It is not the movement, but the rhythm behind the movement that is mirrored. Instead of duplicating his physical movement exactly, you can create a movement of your own that is similar in its speed and duration.

For example, he strokes the back of his chair while you're talking. You rub your glasses in exactly the same rhythm. He taps his fingers. You jiggle your foot in the same rhythm. At the same time, begin to observe his breathing.

Mirroring Breathing

How often have you fallen asleep with a lover in the afterglow of sex and felt yourself breathing in unison? Remember how wonderfully intimate it was when you felt that mutual rhythm as you drifted off? Didn't you feel remarkably close, bathed in an especially warm security, filled with a feeling of togetherness as if you were really becoming one?

What you felt was the same closeness the tantric yogis accomplish during sex, by breathing together in and out in perfect harmony.

What easy magic to recreate! The surprise is that you can do it anywhere. You don't have to wait to get into bed with a man to be close. Start at the first meeting by watching his breathing.

You can tell how quickly or slowly a man is breathing by watching his shoulders. Mark them with a spot on the wall behind him and watch them go up and down. Then simply start breathing yourself in the same rhythm.

If he's a deep slow breather and you're a fast shallow breather, try to adopt his breathing pattern. While he's talking, notice when he takes a breath. Is it often, or just once in a while? You breathe when he does.

Breathing together is one of the really subtle ways to get close. Subconsciously, it reminds a man of when he was safe and secure in his mother's womb. A man always feels trusting of a woman who breathes the way he does.

Notice men working out together with heavy weights. One lifts the weight and two others assist with the weight and urge him on. What's interesting is that the men assisting seem to adopt the weightlifter's breathing pattern.

Go jogging with a lover. Notice how sympatico you feel as you both gasp for air. You are breathing in sync, a very effective mirroring technique for getting close.

You can breathe "in sync" with anyone. It doesn't have to be a lover. Try it on your boss. Or anyone else you want to like you. Breathing in sync is amazingly simple and effective. Learn to use it to your advantage with your lover.

Mirroring Life Rhythms

Some people are night people, some are day people. Some people are full of fun and vigor in the early mornings and some people aren't.

For two years, Susan, a thirty-two-year-old fashion magazine editor, had been dating Ernie, a television cameraman. They spent almost every weekend together and often one night during the week, taking turns staying at each other's houses. Mostly, Susan stayed over with Ernie at his place.

Susan, who had never been married, felt that her biological clock was running out. She wanted to get married and start a family. Ernie, who had been married twice before, was evasive and noncommittal until Susan began to mirror his life rhythm.

In spite of the fact that Ernie grew up on a farm, he was slow in the mornings. He wanted lots of quiet time with his morning newspaper before he did anything.

Susan, on the other hand, was out of bed with the first light of day, and off to jog or play tennis. She really tried to get Ernie interested in joining her, but he made it obvious he would be quite happy if she'd go "do her own thing." Susan didn't want to do her own thing. She wanted to do her thing with Ernie.

At first glance, it would seem that this couple just might not be compatible. But Susan swore she was deeply in love with Ernie and that there was no other man in the world she could love. Even the thought of leaving Ernie made her angry and upset.

"Everything else seems so good with us," she puzzled. "I don't understand why he doesn't want to spend more time with me." The answer was pretty obvious. Susan had been emphasizing the differences between her and Ernie by refusing to slow her morning rhythm down to his.

If she really wanted Ernie, Susan came to realize, she'd have to learn to schedule her tennis game at a later time. She had to slow down and get "in sync" with Ernie's rhythm in order for him to feel like spending more time with her.

Ernie and Susan were soon playing tennis together—over lunchtime. Not in the early morning. Susan was learning to enjoy a morning newspaper with Ernie. In just one month after she changed her morning rhythm to his, Ernie was wanting to spend so much more time with Susan, they became engaged.

In order to become the leader when there is a difference in rhythm between you and a man, in order to get into a state of agreement, you must first match your rhythm to his. Then change slowly, and he'll follow.

To get a man to change, you must first change yourself. Then watch him change his behavior in reaction to the changes in yourself. Getting "in sync" with a man's moods is very important. Then you can get him to change if you want.

Susan got in step with Ernie's moods, his highs and lows and ups and downs. Then she was able to get him to make changes because he immediately became more open to her suggestions when she became more like him. He trusted her more and felt more comfortable around her. He felt that this was indeed a woman he could happily spend the rest of his life with because they were "in sync."

Mirroring Volume

If the man you are interested in is a quiet type, if he rarely shouts or raises his voice above a whisper, you should be quiet too. He'll respond easily to you if you match your volume to his own volume, but he'll draw away if you talk loudly a lot or shout around him. If you're with a man who always talks in mellow, quiet tones, be sure to modulate your own voice.

Sometimes this quiet type of man can make a woman angry because she feels as if he doesn't react. "I wish he'd be more emotional," one woman told me about her quiet artist lover. "Sometimes I'm tempted to do something really outrageous just to get him angry."

She did. Just once, she made a date with her artist lover and when he arrived her ex-husband was there and they were having a loud argument. The artist didn't get involved although she tried to get him to join in. He simply left and didn't see her again for two weeks. He told her he had a big job to finish on a deadline, but she knew that in his quiet way, he was punishing her for making him part of the angry scene. Failing to mirror got her two weeks alone.

On the other hand, you may run into a loud, boisterous man. In order to reach him, you might have to get louder yourself. Once you do, you might even get him to tone down a little as the following example shows.

Jane, a twenty-seven-year-old stewardess, was mad for Stuart, a thirty-four-year-old lawyer. Stuart was loud in even the simplest discussion, and Jane often felt overwhelmed.

"It's not that I even disagree with him," she told me. "It's simply that I don't think he even hears what I say at all.

"For instance, we were discussing the movie *E.T.* and he was saying it wasn't a good movie because if

E.T. could fly all along, he was never in any jeopardy. I had totally enjoyed the movie even though I didn't disagree with him.

"So there he was screaming about the inconsistencies in the film and I felt totally bullied. I couldn't get a word in anyway. So I said, 'I loved the movie,' and he ranted on for another fifteen minutes about what a cheat it was. I was actually afraid even to talk about that movie again."

The next time they were together, Jane tried a simple mirroring technique—she talked louder. The trick she had to learn was to *agree* loudly. Purposely, she brought up the subject of *E.T.,* almost cringing at Stuart's predictable outbreak.

Once again, Stuart began to rant about the Spielberg film, but this time, Jane was ready. "You're right," she screamed back at him and banged on the coffee table with her fist.

"It's a terrible trick for a filmmaker to play on an audience. He should be ashamed of himself. I don't understand why I liked it so much in spite of the inconsistencies and cheap tricks." Again, she banged on the table for emphasis.

Stuart, shocked by her reaction, immediately changed his behavior. "Now, now," he said, his voice hardly above a whisper. "Don't get upset. Take it easy." Suddenly, Stuart was on the receiving side of his own behavior. He didn't like it one bit and changed his own behavior immediately.

You also can change a man's behavior, but first you must be willing to change your own. Then, once you are both "in sync," you can exert your influence on the man. In Jane's case, when she screamed her agreement with Stuart's film criticism, she wasn't just mirroring the volume in Stuart's voice, she was mirroring something else—his belief system.

Mirroring Belief Systems

Surely there must be some idea of his that you agree with absolutely and totally. If not, what are you doing together? Whenever you want to convince your lover of something, start with an area of agreement. Then you can go on to the area of disagreement.

Remember, conflict breeds more conflict. Agreement breeds agreement.

This doesn't mean that you should lie or say things you don't mean. Even the simplest lie can trip you up later.

One thirty-five-year-old woman told her thirty-year-old husband-to-be that she was thirty-three years old, two years younger than her real age. "Lying about your age is traditional," some of her friends told her. "Don't worry about it."

Now they are married and she is constantly worried that he'll turn up an old high school yearbook and find out the truth. She's having trouble getting pregnant and has to lie to the fertility clinic about how old she is. She lives in fear that a hospital record will show her husband her real age. And the longer she puts off telling him, the more upset he's going to be when he finds out.

Lying will only produce a bad relationship and cause problems for you later. Saying things you don't mean will only make you resentful and angry.

Always telling the truth can be difficult, though, especially when we women have been taught that it's perfectly okay to deceive men just a little for the sake of love. But there is a right way and a wrong way to tell a man the truth.

In its simplest form, let's say you are going out with a guy who's just crazy about Chinese food. You like Chinese food too, but not all the time.

Unfortunately, in the beginning of your relationship, you pretended you liked Chinese food just a little more than you really did, to be agreeable. Now you find that he happily takes you out for Chinese food whenever you see each other. How do you break the news?

You don't want to have him suddenly feel foolish for having bought you all those Chinese dinners. But you also think you'll die if you have Chinese food one more time.

This isn't the time to blurt out, "The very thought of another Chinese restaurant makes me want to barf. Can't we get a steak for a change?"

You must learn to control these outbursts, whether they're concerned with sex or Chinese food. Always start from an area of agreement.

Begin by saying something like, "I've been a Chinese food fan all my life. Chinese food is always fresh and full of steamed vegetables, one of my favorites."

At this point, you and your lover are in agreement. Then you can add, "But lately, I've had an overwhelming urge for a steak," or, "I've been thinking a lot about meat and potatoes."

You will have started by mirroring his belief system concerning Chinese food, so he is receptive to your idea. You haven't lied or compromised yourself; you have simply found an agreeable way to start the discussion. Then, when you've gotten him in the pattern of agreement, you can bring up the other food.

Roger and Bernadette had been dating for six months and Bernadette was fed up with his lack of sexual expertise. "He does the same thing all the time," she complained. "I can't even get him to *discuss* anything besides missionary position sex. When I bring up exciting things like oral sex or even another position, he says he enjoys doing just what comes naturally."

Bernadette learned that, instead of directly pushing Roger into a new sex act, she should start from a point of agreement. She began to talk about how the natural way was terrific, and that she had always enjoyed every moment of their lovemaking.

After first assuring Roger that she hadn't been faking it all along, that she really did enjoy his missionary position lovemaking, he was much easier to get into experimental sex. But first she had to start with their point of agreement.

A man is always more reluctant to change than a woman. That's why it's especially important to find his point of agreement and to mirror his belief systems before bringing up new ideas.

Getting into agreement isn't hard. Mirroring belief systems doesn't have to be a big deal. Doctors do it all the time to get close to their patients.

Remember during your last office visit, how she looked at your chart and said, "Let's see, you're twenty-eight," and you nodded agreement? "Never been pregnant," and you agreed again. Then she was able to go on, with you feeling trusting and confident, because she got you into an area of agreement first.

You can agree with a man over anything. You can say, "You like sports," or, "You seem tired." Just getting into agreement with him and then beginning to mirror his belief systems can make him trust you the way a patient trusts a doctor.

There probably are no limits to the amount of mirroring you can do. Let your imagination run wild.

Mirror the rhythm of a lover's sentences, the blinking of his eyes, the way he views his universe, his breathing and his belief systems. He'll be putty in your hands.

Anchoring Your Love

11

WHEN YOU HAVE BEGUN TO ESTABLISH SOME LOVing good feelings with the new man in your life, you will want a way to keep those special warm feelings from going away. That is, you will want to *anchor* those feelings and make them available "on call."

Anchoring Happy Feelings

Just as a touch on the arm is often a comfort to the bereaved or depressed person, and a hug expresses a warm greeting, you can make a special touch remind your lover of the best, most loving feelings in your relationship. If you do your anchoring work right, those good feelings can be restimulated by you at will. Anchoring is a potent tool for making a man fall in love with you.

Here's how anchoring works. Each time you and your lover are especially happy together, you will preserve the moment by anchoring it with a special touch—the same touch each time. After several repetitions, this will become a "happy-times" anchor. Then, at a time when he's grouchy or out of sorts, you can evoke the good times and erase the current bad feelings with this particular touch.

For example, you and a lover are off for a weekend together. Everything is going along perfectly. The day is beautiful. As you leave the house, he says, "Don't you wish every day was this terrific? I love the way the sun shines through the clouds, don't you?"

You say, "Yes, I love this kind of a day too," and you touch a chosen spot on his body in a special way. The special touch could be a tight squeeze of his hand between both of yours, or a little rub on the back of his neck—whatever feels natural and easy to do in different situations of happiness. It really doesn't matter what spot you pick, as long as you don't pick the upper arm—long associated with grief and condolences.

Remember the touch and the spot. Each time he feels really good, repeat this anchoring process, telling him that you too feel good. If he's auditory, be sure to say his name out loud while touching your chosen spot. Soon, good feelings and only good feelings will be associated with that touch and that place on his body.

After a few repetitions, you can try using the "happy-time" anchor to give him (and you) a lift some time when he's down. Remember to mirror his mood first, then once you're "in sync" with him, turn his mood around with the anchor and some appropriate words. For example, "Oh, Honey, I see you're unhappy today, and I understand. But . . ." (now touch the anchor) ". . . it's supposed to be a gorgeous weekend; we'll get out, have fun and forget business for a while."

Anchoring can give you a feeling of control in a relationship and can be helpful in dealing with relationship problems when they occur.

Lynn, an outgoing and happy secretary, was dating Henry, a moody, unpredictable artist. When he was happy his happiness lit up the world around them, but when he was sad, it was as though a black cloud hung over them both.

"If I could just keep him in his good mood and do something about his rotten ones, I'd be happy with our relationship," she said. "I love him so much when he's up. But when he's down, it's as if a tragedy had just happened. He acts like someone died.

"Then when he's depressed, I get depressed, I feel that he should be happy. I mean, there I am, ready to do anything to bring him around. I tell jokes, act silly, even sexy, and he doesn't care. Once I even painted little faces on my tits and he just groaned and got more depressed. Does making a man love you have to be so hard?" she asked me.

The answer was no, it doesn't. Actually, if you have to work so hard all the time, it may be that you have the wrong man. Lynn assured me that she didn't, so she gave up her silly "make him happy" ploys and tried anchoring.

For the next month, Lynn practiced anchoring

Henry's happy feelings. Every time he felt good, she began to massage his hands.

The next time Henry got depressed, Lynn didn't try any of her old tricks to cheer him up. Instead, she mirrored him by saying, "Henry, anyone can see that the account people were fools. They missed the whole point of your presentation." Then she started to massage his hands. "But the hell with them. I love you and we're going to have a wonderful evening." It worked like magic.

Today, Henry still gets depressed, but Lynn can almost always change his mood by activating his happiness anchor.

Whenever you see the man in your life happy, no matter why, kiss his ear, tickle his palm or touch him in some other way that develops a special bond between you. Then, when the good feelings seem to be slipping away, you can bring back the subconscious memory of those feelings by kissing the same ear, tickling the same palm, or giving him that special touch.

Anchoring Sexy Feelings

A sexy anchor is about the easiest and most effective anchor you can establish. Maryanne, a thirty-six-year-old medical instruments saleswoman, was getting desperate because the man she loved had so many other women who loved him too. "I don't know what I'm going to do to stand out in the mob," she told me.

"They buy theatre tickets and take him to first-run plays; they bake cookies and leave them on his doorstep. I know they're all younger than me, thinner than me, and probably better in bed. I've been trying to make an impression, but I just can't seem to get ahead of the crowd."

Instead of trying to outbribe, outcook, or outscrew her competitors, Maryanne tried anchoring. At first she was tentative, but soon she became an expert at it.

"I was really scared he'd find out what I was doing," she said. "But I realized there was no other way I could stand out as a lover.

"So, just as Bob was starting to have his orgasm, I reached up and kissed his neck just below his ear. 'Oh, Bob, Oh Bob,' was about all I could think of to say. As he was coming, I kissed and nuzzled that spot on his neck.

"I tried to do the same anchoring every time we made love. If we weren't face-to-face when he had his orgasm, I would kiss the same spot and say the same words as soon as possible in the warmth and good feelings of our afterglow. Soon, I was able to turn him on wherever we were by simply caressing that spot on his neck and whispering, 'Oh, Bob,' in an especially sexy tone of voice.

"When I did that, he couldn't wait to get me home to bed. It didn't take long before he began to miss that special touching whenever he was out with the other women. Of course, they didn't know the secret.

"I don't know if he ever figured out why he stopped seeing all those other women, but I never told him." Maryanne and Bob are currently married and living in Denver, where she reports that he still gets excited when she touches the side of his neck and says, "Oh Bob"

Anchoring in bed with a lover is very powerful and effective. Try it with your lover. During or right after each orgasm, caress a special spot. You might hold his balls gently, or you could suck his earlobe. It doesn't matter what you do as long as you do something special, and do it consistently.

Very quickly, the touch of that spot, the particular way you do it, and the sensation he gets will become identified with the pleasure only you provide. Soon, by simply touching the pleasure-indicating spot, you can induce the same pleasure without the sex act.

Like Maryanne, you will want to have special words that go with touching his sensitive love anchor spot. Perhaps you would want to say his name, or even something in his Love Language. Use a special tone of voice as well. Soon you can reactivate his sexuality by just using your unique tone of voice or saying the special words.

If your man is a visualizer, you could say, "You look so sexy, I can't resist you." Or, "Seeing you makes me hot." Or, "That look in your eye turns me on."

If he's a feeling type, you might say, "You feel so wonderful." Or, "I love to touch you." Or, "Touching you turns me on."

If he's into the language of sounds, always coo, use your sexiest voice, and say, "Oh (insert name)," or just make up a silly sexy sound like a growl. Growl when you touch him. Or you could say, "It sounds like you're a little horny."

Anchoring to Solve Problems

You can also anchor bad feelings. What, you may wonder, would you want to do that for? Shouldn't you just let the bad feelings go, maybe ignoring them to see if they'll go away?

No, don't ignore bad feelings. That doesn't make them disappear. Anchor bad feelings too. Then you can step away from them. Here's an example:

May, a forty-two-year-old medical secretary, had been dating Peter, an anesthesiologist, for some time. She was madly in love with him and he said he was in love with her too, but there were some real problems in their relationship.

Peter had been married three times before. May had never even gone steady or been engaged. She was ready for commitment long before he was. She yearned to be with Peter on a permanent basis, but Peter was scared by her love.

"He says he loves me, but he's had such bad experiences with women before, he's afraid to get more involved," she told me. "If only I could get Peter to stop associating all those bad memories from the past with me.

"*I* wasn't the one who left him. *I* didn't take all his money in a divorce settlement. *I've* never taken any money from a man and never would; yet he's afraid I'll marry him and then leave him like the others. How can I convince him I'm not like those other women?"

May had already learned to anchor Peter's happy feelings by rubbing his shoulders and talking to him in a warm loving tone of voice in his language, which was visual. She had his good feelings anchor permanently set.

She rubbed and rubbed, saying things like, "I can see us together when we're old and gray," and, "You look so good to me, if I were an artist, I'd paint your picture." Peter loved his good feelings being anchored, but every time she stopped, he was overwhelmed by the memories of how badly he'd been hurt in the past.

"I've told him I'm not like those other women, but he doesn't seem to believe me," said May. She despaired of Peter's ever being able to forget his old pain and enjoy his new relationship.

Then she learned to anchor his bad feelings as well as his good ones. The next time Peter started talking about how badly he'd been hurt and how those other women took his money and his home and how he could never stand to go through another divorce, May didn't argue. In fact, she agreed (mirroring his belief system), and she anchored his bad memories to a spot in the room that was far away from her.

Going over to a chair in the far corner where they never sat, May said, pointing to the chair, "Some women are like that. Those women are the ones who hurt men and just think about what they can get in a relationship."

Then, instead of defending herself as one of the women who "is different," she stepped away from the chair where she had anchored the bad feelings and said to Peter, "Then there are other women who don't treat men badly." As she said this, she put the same hand she had pointed at the chair on her chest.

"Some women," she said, "are different and would never think of loving a man and then leaving him. Some women are loyal and loving and want to grow old with the man they love." She started rubbing his shoulders. "Some women believe in staying together forever."

What May did was anchor his bad feelings to the chair in the corner of Peter's living room, someplace away from herself. Then she had moved physically away from the chair and used the same hand to nonverbally indicate herself as one of those other women who do love forever.

Whenever Peter brought up some pain from his old marriages, May was able to disassociate herself from that pain by anchoring it away from her own body. Soon, she had developed both positive and negative anchors she could use with Peter.

When she disassociated herself from his past and what those other women had done to him, he saw her in a new light, by herself, not as one of the crowd after his assets. Soon they were living together and engaged. It only took her negative anchor of his bad feelings to separate her from his painful past.

Cynthia, a secretary, had the opposite problem with her lover Mark, a printer. Mark was carrying around the past memory of a totally dependent wife. For ten unhappy years he had been married to a woman who lived and died for him. The pressure was intense. He told Cynthia he didn't ever want to get that close to a woman again because he couldn't stand that much dependency.

So Cynthia created a negative anchor about "that" kind of woman. She told Mark, "A lot of men can't handle a woman who is independent and has a life of her own. They need *that* kind of woman."

(She pointed at the space in the room she had just vacated.) "But then there are a lot of women who aren't like that and who don't need to be clinging all the time." (At that point, she used her special tone of voice and touched his good-feelings anchor spot.)

In spite of what we're told about supporting other women, you don't have to support all women all the time—especially when it's important to separate yourself in a man's eyes from another woman's bad behavior. Sometimes it's hard to get over the hurt of the past, but with negative and positive anchoring, you can help your man appreciate your qualities without prejudices formed in the past.

Don't be shy about using a negative anchor. It can give you an almost physical "handle" on a relationship problem, permitting you to deal with it and disassociate yourself from it.

Everyone already has positive and negative anchors. The man you love already has some. For instance, he loves his dog. If you are petting the dog, some of that love will spill over on you.

Or he hates his boss. If you are standing next to his boss at an office party, some of the hate could spill over. Always be sure to position yourself close to the ones he loves. Then you will get automatic spillover from his established anchors.

Getting Him to Do What You Want in Bed

12

"TOUCH MY CLIT, TOUCH MY CLIT," I THOUGHT, pounding my pubis against Bob's as I imagined the word *clit,* hoping I could send a mental message to the gorgeous hunk in my bed.

"If he would only touch my clit, I knew I would come. But he didn't. He lay there with his erect penis buried deep inside me, his hands playing with my tits, my ass, my lips, but acting as if my clit didn't exist. I would have said something, but I'd had bad reactions from lovers in the past when I spoke up and asked for what I wanted."

My friend Penny was telling me the story of herself and her lover Bob. She later found out that Bob was one of those men who feel that if two people are really in love, really in tune with each other, they shouldn't *have* to tell each other what they want in bed. They should each know automatically what the other one wants.

Penny was rightfully afraid that if she started telling Bob what to do, he'd lose his erection, the spontaneity and excitement would die, and he'd start thinking about finding a less bossy, more "natural" lady. Unfortunately, nothing was being done to improve their sex life.

Penny and Bob had already known each other for four months, and their sexual desires weren't even close to harmonious. Frequently, she found herself pretending that she was enjoying their lovemaking more than she really was. She also found herself fantasizing about lovers she used to have and missing their lust. Bob was gentle and kind as a lover and a person, but Penny wanted him to make love to her with hard driving strokes, to ravish her until she couldn't stand it anymore.

Instead, he'd always use a soft touch. He'd never grab her and fulfill her fantasies. She began to feel guilty because she was never quite satisfied. In her imagination, she would be making love to someone else, not Bob. Sometimes she'd take Bob's hand and try to force it toward her clit, silently giving signals she hoped he would read.

Instead, Bob seemed almost purposely not to make love the way she wanted him to. Penny, of course, had read the books that say, "Ask for what you want in bed. Don't be shy. Men love you to tell them what you like in bed." This conflicted with some of her past experiences, but when she finally got desperate, she tried it.

As soon as she began making requests of Bob he

went into a sex slump, ignoring her desires, performing less and less frequently, and making it impossible for either one of them to be satisfied. She thought maybe she should be even more explicit, and that just made matters worse. Penny thought their relationship was over. Bob was furious.

"Higher, lower, bigger circles, harder, deeper, touch this, do that. I don't ever want to hear any more directions from you," he told her. "Especially not in bed. I feel like I'm sleeping with a backseat driver."

To keep the relationship alive, Penny quickly backtracked, said it wasn't important, and went back to pretending she was pleased with Bob in bed. But Bob's manhood had been questioned and he was unhappy. She, of course, was unsatisfied, depressed, and despairing. The love affair was on the rocks when she came to me, as a friend, for help.

Pillowtalk That Works

By following The Love Plan, Penny learned to give "safe" suggestions with generalized instead of specific pillowtalk. Penny learned that, deep down, most men retain some insecurities about their sexual prowess, even if they're very accomplished lovers.

When a woman makes a direct request for something new or different in bed, many men will interpret this as a complaint about their adequacy. Bob was one of these. Other men feel a pressure to perform whatever a woman wants, and this always backfires if they can't live up to her expectations.

Penny also learned that, despite her best intentions, it was a mistake to ask Bob to talk about his own private fantasies and secret desires. Each time she did, Bob would go on the defensive. "What is this, a mandatory confessional?" he would say. Penny would be confused and hurt, not realizing that Bob felt she was "putting him on the spot."

Since Bob already felt that Penny was being judgmental about his sexual performance, he was sure that she was going to be judgmental about his fantasies, too. He was worried that they would either seem too tame, betraying an innate lack of sexuality, or they would sound too wild for him to live up to. Confessing fantasies, in Bob's view, was a no-win situation.

Penny, who was about to give up, could hardly believe the solution was so simple. Bob, as a feelings person, loved to sunbathe. The next time they were sunbathing alone together, feeling very relaxed and mellow, she casually remarked, "I just finished reading *A Secret Garden*—it's about women's fantasies. I'm not sure I agree with all of it. . . . What do *you* think most women fantasize about?" Penny was holding her breath, but Bob came back just as casually, "Gee, I don't know. What's the book say?" He was dying to know.

When Penny asked Bob to speculate with her about what *other* women were secretly wishing for in bed, she eliminated the performance pressure and anxiety he had been feeling. For the first time, Penny and Bob had an open, relaxed conversation about sex. Then, after he became comfortable discussing women's fantasies, she was able to ask him what he thought most men secretly desire.

"It was amazing. Whatever Bob said most men

wanted turned out to be exactly what *he* wanted," Penny reported. In turn, Penny made sure she told Bob what all women wanted—which was, of course, what *she* wanted.

Bob and Penny, like most people, found it easier to talk about sex by talking about other people first, then about themselves. Once they found a way over this barrier, they naturally began to feel safer and closer. Soon, even their most secret fantasies came out.

"I told Bob I liked to be spanked during sex," said Penny. "And he told me he liked to have his nipples kissed, but had never had the nerve to ask a woman to do it for him because he thought only women were supposed to be aroused by nipple stimulation."

Confessing her secret desires to Bob in a conspiratorial, rather than a demanding, way made it easier for him to tell her his. You will find that the more you tell the man about your sexuality (with discretion in the beginning, but revealing more as you get close), the more he will tell you about his. Soon Bob and Penny were sharing secrets with each other that no one else knew.

Mutual sharing of intimate secrets automatically makes people feel close. Just don't share too much until you've read Chapter Thirteen, "How Much to Give and How Soon."

Sexual Teasing

Once Penny had discovered how sensitive Bob's nipples were, she started teasing him in a sexual way at odd times, like when they were standing in line at the movies or during a dinner party.

"Do you like to have your nipples bitten?" she would whisper in his ear, sure he'd never thought of it. "What if I twist your nipples when you're coming?" Penny said suggestively. Penny could soon make Bob's erection grow and grow no matter where they were.

Sexy pillowtalk is often exciting outside the bedroom. It is also less threatening because you and your partner don't feel obligated to perform the particular sex act right then. But it does carry over into the bedroom.

The more you talk about your fantasies, even at the supermarket or the movies, the more you are likely to get them. Penny told Bob about her rape fantasies and he was soon a little rougher in bed. His soft touch was still there, but when Penny got excited Bob learned to pound her in the raucous kind of wanton sex she wanted. In turn, she'd voraciously attack his nipples, giving him exactly what he wanted.

"How does that feel?" she'd ask coyly, knowing Bob was entirely into his feelings. Or she'd say, "That feels good. That feels wonderful," over and over again. It was all she could think of, but it worked as if she were Scheherazade whispering erotic tales to him. Bob and Penny are still together, and they are one of the sexiest couples I know.

If Bob had been visual, Penny might have said, "Can you see what I'm doing to your nipples?" Or, "Watch me kiss you all over."

If Bob had been a hearing man, she could have

said, "It sounds like you're turned on." Or, "I can hear that you like that."

Show and Tell

Once you are used to getting exactly what you want in bed, it's hard to adjust to something else. June, a computer programmer, was distraught over her marital breakup.

"Jerry and I were into elaborate fantasies," she told me. "I was a belly dancer and he was dressed as a sultan. We played Patty Hearst and the kidnappers. One time I was a nun captured by heathens. Another time he was an oil executive held by South American rebels. Sometimes one of us pretended to be an animal. How can I get men I date to go along with any of that stuff? They'll think I'm crazy if I even suggest it."

June's new male friends may have been willing to do anything she wanted in bed, but she just didn't have the nerve to confess her elaborate fantasies, especially outside of the bedroom. She was a prim and proper, clean-cut looking woman. Nobody would imagine from seeing her that she ever had sex any way but missionary style. The truth was she was bored with all the men she was meeting and couldn't imagine how to turn any of them into the kind of lover she wanted.

The solution to June's problem was in the sexy book store. She bought erotic magazines with photographs of people engaging in the elaborate fantasies she loved. Then she began showing the magazines to the new men in her life.

"I showed them the books and photos as if I were

doing some kind of elaborate critical study of them, not as if I really wanted to do those things myself. 'What do you think is the turn-on here?' I asked. Soon they'd do exactly what I wanted and sometimes even more."

By learning to verbalize about sex, by asking questions about how others (not you and your partner) view erotic acts, you will be able to establish an aura of openness concerning sex, of being able to talk freely with no repercussions.

Always start pillowtalk somewhere other than the bedroom. It's less threatening that way. Pillowtalk in bed makes a man feel as if he has to perform exactly what you ask immediately. The pressure can be very destructive.

The next time you have an urge for your lover to do something special, don't push his hand or try to squirm into position. Instead, think about fantasizing together in a generalized way about what turns on other people. If books, movies, or articles help you get into the subject, use them. Then talk together about what turns on other people of the opposite sex, then the same sex, then about what turns you on. Talk about sex outside of bed.

Getting Him in the Mood

There's nothing worse than when you are hot and he's not. Sure, you can put on soft music or sexy clothes. You can coddle and beg and coo and seduce. But sometimes it just doesn't work. In spite of your best efforts, he's simply unresponsive. He has a headache, or he's upset.

It's not your fault, but somehow you feel as

though you're to blame. You blame yourself because you're not sexy enough, or you're too fat or too thin, or you said the wrong thing and turned him off. That simply isn't true.

You didn't turn him off, he turned himself off. Maybe he's got his mind on his upcoming performance review at the office, or maybe his mother called and wants him to visit. You really don't need to know for sure, because there is a simple technique you can use to remedy the situation.

What do you say to a man who's not in the mood? How do you get him to feel sexy? By using a variation of the anchoring technique you learned in Chapter Eleven.

Let's say you've just been out with a terrific man and you feel really turned on but some little voice tells you he's not. You can tell he really likes you, but he's just not feeling sexy at the moment.

You sense that he has other things on his mind, which isn't very flattering at this point in the evening. Your self-esteem begins to falter. You wonder if you should just go hide in the back of your closet with a blanket or chalk up one more platonic evening when you feel hot as hell.

There's no need to chalk it off, or to just sit there while he remains polite but distracted. You can get him in the mood with a special anchoring technique I call "Method Sex."

"Method Sex"

"Method" actors prepare for a performance by remembering life experiences of their own that are similar to those of the character they are playing. By getting in touch with that memory anchor just before performing, they are not just acting, but "reliving" those experiences on stage.

In the same way the method actor remembers a past sad experience to portray sadness, you can get your man to remember a past sex experience to feel sexy. Try stimulating his memory.

Ask him to remember a time when he was really turned on. Ask him if he can remember his first sexual experience, or his most exotic.

Watch the expression on his face. Look for an easing of tension around the mouth and eyes. Perhaps a slight smile. It may take a few questions before he really gets into the subject. Meanwhile, remember the What and How questions.

Sometimes a man just won't talk about his past affairs, but you can tell from the expression on his face that he is remembering. He doesn't necessarily have to say a word for "Method Sex" to get him in the mood. (If you're a keen observer, you'll be able to remember your lover's "in lust" expression and file it away for future reference.)

The minute you see signs that he is actually remembering a former sexual experience, *anchor* his feeling and that memory. Touch his hand, or use any of the anchoring techniques explained in the last chapter. By getting him to remember past sexually satisfying times in his life, you will not only be putting him in the mood for sex in the present, you will be creating a useful sexual anchor.

If he's willing to talk about his experiences, this anchoring becomes easy. Just as he reaches the most exciting part of his reminiscences, anchor his thrill. After a few times, you will easily be able to get him to recall the same feeling by repeating the anchor. You won't have to get him to actually recall the experience each time.

Your anchor will be most effective if it is complemented by a statement in his Love Language. If he's a visual man, touch him and say, "I can see why that gave you a fantastic thrill." If he's an auditory man say, "I can hear how exciting that was for you." If he is a feelings man say, "I can understand how good you felt."

Of course, if he isn't responding verbally, you will be limited to whatever effect one or two questions might have. Don't press and don't appear to be interrogating him. Unfortunately, his unwillingness to talk about his past sexual activities and love affairs limits your ability to translate the "Method Sex" into a firm sexual anchor.

Different moods can be created by using different memory anchors. Just as recalling past sex experiences can put him in the mood for sex, recalling past love experiences can put him in the mood for loving. By getting him to remember times when he was happily in love, you will put him in the mood to be in love in the present, with you.

Some women are afraid to ask a man about his past love affairs, particularly about the sexual experiences. They don't want to know, or find it embarrassing to ask, or want to pretend there were never any other women in his life before.

Getting your man to recall past sexual or love experiences shouldn't be thought of as a threat to your present relationship, no matter how great he says it was. I have known women so insecure that they were threatened even by a man's memory of a deceased lover.

If he's had good experiences with other women, it shows he's capable of having a good experience with you—*especially* if you're listening and learning. Ask him why it was so good, what was it that he liked the best, and what *she* did that was really special. You're much better off if you know everything.

How Much to Give and How Soon

13

"I GAVE HIM EVERYTHING AND HE STILL DIDN'T love me," is a story I've heard over and over again from women. I know exactly what they mean. I've certainly felt that way myself.

There are several reasons why we women feel we have to *give* everything. We've been brought up by a generation of mothers who gave their all to our fathers. We've been taught to be the nurturers of society, the nurses, the teachers, the caretakers. Besides, if we give everything, we think, then the man will take care of us.

Men, on the other hand, are taught that they have to work hard for what they get. Men go out into the world and do battle on a daily basis. They enjoy the fight of working hard for something and then achieving that goal.

Giving Too Much Too Soon

The problem with giving a man everything in the beginning of a relationship is that he doesn't have anything to work for, to achieve. That doesn't mean that you can't go out with a man, make love with him, even live with him—but there must be something more he'll get if he marries you or makes a commitment to you. Otherwise, what's his motivation? There's no challenge.

Helen, a successful motion-picture-studio executive, was a woman who had everything. At only thirty-four years old she had already acquired a house in the hills with a swimming pool and a view of all of Los Angeles. Her house was filled with artwork and fine furniture. She travelled around the world and could afford the best clothes and the fanciest cars—all of which she had. But Helen didn't have a committed relationship and she was really unhappy about the lack of love in her life.

"I don't understand why some guy doesn't jump at the chance of a relationship with me," she bemoaned her single fate. "I have so much to offer."

At first I didn't understand it either. Helen was really a knockout. She had long, dark hair that framed her face like a lion's mane. Her figure was as good as any starlet's and she was always perfectly groomed and coiffed. But later, after I began to listen to the story of her recently failed relationship, and the one before that, I began to understand the reason for Helen's failure to find a love.

Helen was suffering from a severe case of "good girl syndrome." While living a modern and sophisticated big-city life, she was also trying to be the perfect traditional "good girl."

To Helen, being a perfect "good girl" meant that she could only be lovers with one man at a time. Being a good girl also means that she had to try for a "falling in love" relationship with every man she went to bed with.

After all, good girls only go to bed with a man they're serious about, she thought. In order to see herself as a good girl, to justify the sex she wanted, Helen always gave too much too soon. She cooked gourmet dinners for the man she dated, bought him clothes, made plans, bought theatre tickets and was always available. No matter how unfulfilling the relationship, Helen had to be faithful. Frantically she worked at showing each man what a perfect wife she would be.

The men Helen dated were scared off without her knowing why. After a few dates, just as a man was getting seriously interested in his pursuit of Helen, the pursuit was suddenly over, consummated. Helen would be his—body and soul, and heart. She was ready to give her all, the way a good girl does.

Only that was more than the man had bargained for—at least at that stage of their relationship. Helen failed to understand that, despite her good intentions, her rush to commit her love could turn an intriguing affair into a heavy, almost threatening situation for the man.

Men generally have two reactions to this situation. Some will take advantage of the sex and the other offerings while being extra careful not to "get in too deep." The relationship has nowhere to go, the guy soon gets bored, and he moves on. The other reaction is for a man to really worry about why so much is being offered so soon, chalk it up to extreme neediness, and leave immediately.

Neediness Turns Men Off

By offering everything too soon, Helen seemed needy. There's nothing that will turn a healthy man off sooner than a really needy woman.

The worst impression you can give a man is that there is nobody else in your life. Men are competitive by nature. If he can't compete for you, he's likely to find a more challenging woman, one he'll have to fight for.

That's what kept happening to Helen. Her relationships never lasted more than six months. By the time six months were over, the man had more of Helen than he ever wanted, and he was off looking for someone a little harder to get.

Remember the old adage, "Play hard to get." It's partially true. Only instead of *playing* hard to get you should *be* hard to get. Practice turning him down.

The next time he asks you out, tell him you'd love to see him but you already have plans. That's what you'd do if you really are busy and not too eager. And that's what will perk his interest. A man wants a woman who is popular and hard to get. He wants to feel he has a prize other men want—not someone nobody cares about.

See more than one man, especially if you're interested in a serious relationship. If there is one special man you are interested in, you will need to have lots of men in your life, just to keep Mr. Right's attention. You don't have to go to bed with them all if you don't want to; he'll think you did anyway.

"Then the man I want won't have any respect for me," Helen worried when I told her she had to diversify. "He'll think I'm loose and easy."

Soon Helen began to realize that in truth she had been too easy all along, that she actually gave too much for too little. Finally she decided to take matters into her own hands. She joined a dating service. She couldn't believe the change in the men she knew.

The minute her current, couldn't-care-less lover found out Helen was coming to the attention of thousands of eligible men, he became suddenly very attentive. By then, Helen realized she didn't want him. She was already dating lots of other men—and starting out on the right foot in her new relationships.

The Danger of Overromanticizing Too Soon

By the second date you both say, "I love you." By the third date you're talking every night for hours. By the second week you're writing love notes to each other on a daily basis. So where do you go from there? Only down.

Beth and Tony fell in love instantly. They were inseparable after one date. He bought flowers; she cooked dinners every night. He read love poems out loud to her. She always put love notes in his jacket pocket when he went to work.

Then one time he forgot the flowers. Beth was crushed. Then she forgot the note. Tony felt unloved.

Beth and Tony made the fatal relationship mistake of getting totally romantic too soon. The first time one of them missed a romantic gesture, the other one felt cheated and unloved.

If you become totally romantic in love right away, your relationship can only get worse, not better. Relationships, like many other things, either get better or worse. They don't stay the same. Start yours on a low romantic note. Begin as a friend, then build slowly.

If Tony hadn't bought Beth a bouquet every time from the beginning, she would have been thrilled if he showed up with one rose on their fifth date. Instead she was crushed because he forgot one time.

If Beth hadn't left those little notes every time they parted, he would have been thrilled to get one note occasionally.

Too many "I love you"s repeated too soon, too much romantic billing and cooing too soon, spell relationship trouble. Save your love goodies and dole them out like the treasures they are. You'll get a lot more in return. He'll think your "I love you" is more special because it's harder to get.

Time Wasters

Always remember, once you have messed up a relationship with a man, it's almost impossible to get it right again. The advice in this book is meant for new relationships, although I strongly recommend you practice on your old ones.

Your relationship with a man can always improve, but a man will hardly ever turn from Mr. Wrong to Mr. Right. Don't waste your time hoping for miracles.

Finding the right man is never a simple matter, but you won't be free to look as long as you're still trying to make it work with a loser. Helen became successful with relationships once she learned to stop throwing herself at men. But she had to make a fresh start in a whole new direction.

How Much to Tell

One way women often give too much is by telling too much about themselves right away. No man wants to know how your mother or father mistreated you on the first date. He probably doesn't want to hear about it on the third or fourth date either. Nor does he need to know how lousy your last relationship was. He'll think you're a victim and be tempted to make you his victim too.

The best policy is to keep quiet about yourself, revealing only those things you think are important and will get the man you want to reveal something about himself. Don't tell things about yourself just for the sake of talking or out of a need for self-revelation.

Jill, a nursing supervisor, had a serious problem with men. She gave too much too soon and she talked too much. It didn't take more than one date and a man knew more than he ever wanted to know about her. Jill was a total giver.

Men were perfectly content to accept casual sex from her as long as she continued giving. When she wanted a commitment or marriage, though, the answer was always, "I don't understand why we can't go on the way we are." The men were always content. They already had everything Jill had to offer.

When you talk to a man, talk with a purpose. For example, if you want to get close, don't just babble on about yourself. You may say the one thing that will kill the relationship before it starts. One woman always told men about her million-dollar palimony suit left over from her last relationship. She finally learned that some things are better kept to oneself.

Talk to a man about the things that interest him. Be sure to use the Love Language techniques described in Chapters Six, Seven, and Eight. Pick up on his favorite phrases and expressions.

Brenda was dating Ralph, a man she thought had possibilities as a husband. He was a terrific lover and they seemed to get along well.

Ralph met all Brenda's requirements, except that he was a computer programmer and she was deeply involved in the human potential movement. She would have loved him to go to a "Mind-Body-Universe" festival. He'd love to go to a computer show. She wanted to talk about past lives therapy. He wanted to discuss data bases and bytes.

Instead of insisting that he hear about her latest discoveries in the world of the growth movement, she began to learn about computers from him. Soon, she was able to draw a fairly accurate analogy between the computer and the human brain. By the time she began to explain the things she was interested in to Ralph, Brenda was able to use words and phrases he understood.

By mirroring his own words and understanding his computerese, Brenda got "in sync" with Ralph. Then he began to relate to her, and she was able to get him to be more interested in the things she was interested in.

Soon Ralph was making new discoveries in the human potential field and sharing them with Brenda. By first following his lead, she was then able to become the leader. When Ralph felt understood, he was able to accept her ideas better. Once he felt secure in a good relationship, he was more confident about expanding his own horizons.

When Overgiving Starts

How will you know when you've given too much too soon?

When you feel uncomfortable about what you're getting back, you've given too much.

If you have given a man too much too soon, you will expect a lot back. When you don't get back as much as you've given, you'll begin to feel angry and deprived.

You cry for no apparent reason. You're anxious all the time about whether he's going to call. You worry constantly about "other women." These are all signs that you have given too much too soon. Your man is not responding and you'll feel it.

If that happens, if you accidentally give too much before it's time, if you slip and say, "I love you" too soon, or blurt out, "When are you going to call again?" or, "Are we going out Saturday night?" by mistake, then you will have to pull away if you want to keep the man. You'll have to pull further away from him than he did from you.

Take a trip with a girl friend. Go somewhere exotic for two weeks. Send him only *one* postcard. Or, throw yourself into your work for about a month. It won't hurt.

You must give him a chance to miss you. Men don't fall in love with women they don't miss. If you're there all the time, he won't be able to fantasize about you.

Fantasy is one of the most important ingredients of love. A man who is in love has aggrandizing fantasies about the woman he loves.

Ask a man who's in love to tell you about "her." You'll be amazed at how much more beautiful he thinks she is than she really is. You'll wonder how he can think she's so brilliant, so movie star perfect. That's because he's fantasizing, making her bigger than life so he can love her even more.

We've all heard that love is blind. Love isn't blind. It's fantasizing. Lovers since love began have been portrayed as pining away somewhere plucking the petals from flowers and thinking about their love object. If you want to be the love object, you have to give the man time to think about you, to fantasize—without your being there.

I remember the times when men fell in love with me almost instantly. It seems these relationships with some very handsome and intelligent men bloomed best when I was off somewhere right after we met. Or even if the man had to go somewhere that separated us. The reason was that the separation gave us time to fantasize about each other.

Two months after I started dating my husband regularly, I went to Romania as a guest of the Romanian government to research youth treatments. He was left to worry about what I was doing gallivanting behind the Iron Curtain. Actually, my trip was sexless, but he imagined me cavorting with Romanian lotharios the whole time I was gone.

He also had plenty of time to miss me and fantasize about me. He even got a chance to overdose on other ladies. Since I wasn't around, I always came out more favorably than the competition. He had only the fantasy me to compare with the real them. Being unavailable helped make me seem more interesting and desirable.

Separation almost always does make the heart grow fonder, later on in your relationship, as well in the beginning. Always plan some time apart.

GIFTS

Put off giving gifts as long as possible. Show you care in other ways. Give him a massage, or make dinner for him, sew his missing button, or feed his dog when he's out of town. Help him with his kids, his relatives, his problems. But don't give him expensive gifts.

One man told me, "The minute a woman starts giving me valuable things, I feel pressured. She looks like a needy woman who's trying to buy love. When a woman gives me something expensive, it makes me feel as if an alien element has come into the relationship—the element of dollar value as opposed to love and caring. I also feel forced to keep up in some way."

If you feel you must give a gift, make it something with little monetary value. Don't try to impress him with how much you've spent. Instead, let him see how creative you can be without spending a lot.

No man wants to live the rest of his life with a spendthrift. Giving him an expensive gift (even for his birthday or Christmas) will just make him worry about how you'll spend his money if the two of you get married.

Unfixable Loves

If you have given too much too soon, and you sense he's pulling away, you're already on the downslope of the relationship and the situation is irretrievable. That's the price of giving too much too soon.

If that happens, *immediately* begin looking for someone new. Don't waste your time on a man who doesn't want you. With The Love Plan, you have the power to create a truly mutual, loving relationship, but only if you start out right. It's very hard, if not impossible, to salvage a love that has already gone downhill.

Relationships either improve or get worse. If you're involved in one that's getting worse, you should extricate yourself from it as soon as possible and start over.

This time, don't give too much too soon. Don't say, "I love you," before he does, just to force his hand. Don't ask him to forsake all others for you.

Those acts have to be voluntary—but you *can* set up an atmosphere that will make him more likely to volunteer.

Winning with Giving

The very latest studies on love have come up with an interesting aspect of the "in love" feeling. The man who falls in love will have to have his love returned somewhat, but not entirely. He has to have hope of having it returned all the way in the future.

The meaning of this research is clear. Until the relationship has matured and mutual commitment is definite, you should never be the one to say "I love you" all the time, and you shouldn't even say it back every time he does. You should be somewhat available, but not available whenever he wants you.

You should let him know you care about him, but you shouldn't call him on the phone every single night just to chat. Skip a night or two. Call intermittently. Don't send him every adorable card you find. Don't bake his favorite oatmeal raisin cookies for him on every visit.

If you are totally available, if you make all the sexual advances, if you are the one always asking him out, then you are on the road to relationship suicide. You must cut it out immediately.

Gladys, an old friend, was dating Fred whom she felt was "just shy." Or maybe, she insisted, "he simply has a low sex drive." Or, "It's because he's going to school and he's so worried about his studies, I have to make all our social arrangements." Or, "I cook for him all the time because he doesn't have time to cook or money to take us out."

Whatever she did for Fred was because of some problem he had that made it necessary. From Fred's point of view everything was terrific. He had his love returned totally—but he wasn't in love with Gladys.

Unfortunately, she was in love with Fred.

But Gladys had set up an impossible situation. Fred *couldn't* fall in love with her. He never got a chance to miss her, and he never got a chance to fantasize about her. He never got a chance to wonder if she'd one day return his love fully. She already did.

You must use self-control on your urges to give. The reason is that you want to set up a situation where the man has to do something to get you—not where you work hard to get him. The relationship *must* have somewhere to go; you must give it time to develop.

Never overwhelm a man by giving too much too soon, because that's psychologically bad for the future success of your relationship. Perhaps the hardest thing is to do nothing in a relationship, but often it's the only sound thing to do. The best way to keep a man coming back is to dole out little bits of you at a time, just enough to keep him interested but not too much. Always leave him wanting more of you—not relieved that you're gone.

There are very sound psychological principles behind returning a man's affection less than totally—especially in the beginning of a relationship. Being rewarded once in a while, somewhat unpredictably, makes men and women work harder to achieve a prize. If you're clever, you can use this information to make a man really want you, and work hard to win you.

Sit back, relax. Let him come to you. He will, because you know the secrets of reaching out to him without seeming needy.

Why Indifference Works

Have you ever noticed how women who treat men with absolute negligence and disdain often have men fighting for their attention? Have you ever noticed how a man you've treated with indifference keeps coming back again and again? It's because you haven't shown him that you are crazy about him.

Instead, you've been nice once in a while, out of pity, perhaps. You've given him very little encouragement and yet he calls you constantly, wants to buy you presents, do things for you, take you out.

The dollops of niceness you've doled out to some nerd you don't care about can make him crazy with devotion for you. It's easy when you don't care. The hard part is acting a little indifferent when you care a lot.

It takes self-control to keep from throwing yourself at a man when you spot Mr. Right. But don't do it. You'll just scare him away.

Sticking to The Love Plan for getting the man you want is sometimes as hard as sticking to a diet, sometimes even harder. If you feel tempted to do the wrong thing, to call him on a made-up excuse he'll see right through, develop an understanding with a friend who will be supportive.

Use the buddy system and call your friend when you feel tempted to blow it with a man you're interested in. The phone is so easy. His number keeps going through your head. You must resist! One phone call too many or one winsome gift too many can ruin everything you've worked hard to establish.

Breaking old habits isn't easy, but when they're bad love habits, breaking them can be more than worthwhile. If you've had trouble with relationships, learning not to give too much too soon can mean the difference between success and failure.

When to Give Your All

When he gives his all, you give yours. If he has made a commitment and you have too, if you've mutually decided this is it, if you've become an exclusive couple, then you should be almost totally giving.

No matter how much you give, there will always be a private part of you that's just you, your core. That's the part you can never give away. It may be just ten percent, but it's you. Treasure it.

Assuring Return Engagements

14

ONE OF THE MOST IMPORTANT PARTS OF FALLING in love is getting the man to want to see you over and over again. You don't want to throw yourself at him (as we just discussed in Chapter Thirteen), but neither do you want to leave it entirely up to him to remember you, think of something to do together, and then call you. Some men are just plain busy. Many others have trouble thinking of something to do on a date and won't call until they do.

There are lots of ways a woman can take the initiative. Some are better than others.

There's the sexy phone call routine. You call and say, "I've just gotten a magnum of champagne and I'm dying to open it, but I don't have anyone to share it with." Or, "I've been thinking about how sexy you are all day long." This sort of thing always worked for Lauren Bacall in the movies. It might work for you, but there are drawbacks.

First of all, the sexy phone call is almost unavoidably a "right now" proposition. Nothing wrong with being spontaneous (if you really are), but what if he has other plans for that evening? If he does, you'll both wind up feeling awkward. Second, the sexy phone call is not real subtle, and you run the risk of sounding a bit desperate.

Or there's the ploy of "accidentally" leaving something you need desperately so he'll have to see you again soon just to return the treasure. For instance, your address book, or your briefcase, or your only winter coat, or your entire makeup kit. Surely no man would be so coldhearted as to deny you the return of your needed belongings, and if you wind up in bed during the return, all the better.

The problem is he often knows exactly what's going on. Or your ploy could backfire. I remember once when I was dating my husband, another woman he had been seeing "accidentally" left her address book at his apartment. He was too busy the next day to return it, so he offered to leave it out under a pot where he always kept his spare front-door key. She was to stop by during the day to pick it up but, as it turned out, she didn't get a chance. As it also turned out, I was to meet him at his apartment for a date that evening and he was running late. So while letting myself in with the hidden key, I found the book. I had plenty of time to check out the other woman's address book and she was embarrassed when her obvious ploy didn't work out.

Other times, women would leave their belongings at his place and I would wind up using them. Do you want some other women using your "accidentally" left hairbrush, makeup or perfume? Of course not.

Some women send cute cards, or leave little gifts like special cookies or bread they've baked. While still not subtle, this ploy is less aggressive and a lot smarter. These women are on the right track. A man, when rereading your card, or eating the cookies you've baked, will naturally think of you—and favorably.

Some gifts function as gifts only; some do double duty as "memory triggers." The Love Plan will teach you memory triggers that are far more subtle and powerful than cards or cookies. An effective memory trigger will make him think of you in the right way—so strongly that he will want to see you again. He will pick up the phone and call you. That is the goal.

Subtle Triggers

A memory trigger doesn't even have to be a gift. Consider a spray of your favorite perfume, sneaked onto his inner pillow or sprayed around his mattress. He smells it and thinks of you. Your special soap in the shower. He washes with it and thinks of you.

You know your lover's Love Language. The love triggers you will use to remind him of you when you're not around will be directly related to his Love Language. With a visual lover, you'd want to leave things around for him to see. For example, a "coffee-table" book you know he likes. Whenever he sees it he thinks of you. Equally subtle and effective would be a picture you bought together that hangs on his wall, a special dried flower arrangement, a video game you play together.

With a hearing man, you'll want to leave the sounds of love. Maybe a favorite record with your favorite song or recording artist. A melody you like to harmonize together. Wind chimes you bought together. A special kind of telephone bell. Stereo headphones.

With a feelings man, you'll want to leave sensual memories. Something he can touch, or smell, or taste. Home-baked cookies aren't bad, but they're soon gone. Try a bottle of aftershave you've picked out especially for him. Or a new razor that's specially made or well balanced. Take him shopping for a new lounging robe in exactly the fabric he feels most comfortable in. Anything he'll use often and react to sensually when he does.

Of course, if you think of a subtle, surefire trigger that doesn't happen to be in his Love Language, use it anyway. Remember that although a man operates primarily in one Love Language or another, he can be triggered by the others too.

Building an Instant History

In order for love to bloom, as we've pointed out before, there has to be fantasy. He's more likely to fantasize about you if your relationship has developed its own history, complete with wonderful memories. The Love Plan will show you how to create an "Instant History."

Memories are made of wonderful moments you

two have together. It's important that there be a buildup of loving good times, of things you've done together that create lasting memories. That's the history of a relationship. The times you've loved, the times you've laughed, even the times you've cried together, all make up the memories of you he can recall when you're not around.

You can "create" such a history. You don't have to wait for years of incidents, of trips you take together, or unusual things you do. Start planning an Instant History for you and the man you love. Don't wait for the memories to build; create them.

Find a favorite singer who has a meaningful song that the two of you like. Be sure to take him to a performance. Make the night a memorable event with something special—for instance, a dinner at a restaurant in an unusual location, or with a special kind of food or service. Or you might make the night memorable by renting a room in an X-rated motel afterward. Or you might rent a limo to take you both to a concert.

Instant History can be created with imagination. Even without spending much money, you can figure out memorable things to do with the man you love. Perhaps you take him on a mystery date where nothing's really expensive, but everything's a surprise, or you stage an especially erotic seduction, or you arrange a "potluck" birthday dinner party for him with all of his friends.

Remember the things men did with you that you'll never forget. The time someone took you for a helicopter ride, or the swap meet where he bought you a puppy. Or the time he taught you to use his soldering iron. Those are the kinds of moments that make up the history of a relationship.

Take advantage of opportunities to create Instant History. Help him to move. Rescue a stray dog or cat and find a home for it together. Take him to a family picnic or event.

When Sylvia, a twenty-eight-year-old department store buyer and amateur photographer, met Monty, she knew she'd found her man. Following The Love Plan, Sylvia discovered that Monty, a divorced, thirty-year-old fireman, was highly visual. She knew she had to take her time with Monty, but she was smart enough to document their entire relationship with snapshots, including some of her and his little boy together.

As the relationship developed, she shared the snapshots with Monty. Soon the photos became a little scrapbook—a visual Instant History. Later, after Sylvia and Monty were married, he confessed to her that he "used to look at that damn scrapbook a dozen times a day" when they were apart.

Always plan an Instant History for any new man you're serious about. Think in terms of memories—they'll always trigger love.

The Podium Effect

One important quality of love is admiration. It is also the precursor to love. We admire people whom other people admire. One way to gain a man's admiration (and to assure return engagements) is to show him how much other people love and admire you.

Instead of trying to explain to a man that I was a

respected author and lecturer, I often invited new men I was dating to watch me give a television interview or a lecture. They always admired me more after they saw me behind a podium with other people looking up to me.

You don't have to be on television to create the Podium Effect, either. For example, invite him to come along when your team plays for the company softball championship, or the bowling league title. Or consider inviting him to a big party where you have assembled all of your oldest and closest and most loving friends. You'll be amazed at how the admiration your friends have for you rubs off on him.

Be sure to say some nice things about him to your gathered friends, "anchor" the occasion with him, and you will have also created a special memory to contribute to your Instant History.

Repetition

Understanding the factors that make love a habitual, necessary part of a man's life can help you secure your love relationship. You can become a habit with him, if you know how habits are formed.

One of the main ways both men and women form habits is by repetition. Any act, repeated in the same way over and over again, becomes a habit, a minor addiction.

Have you ever noticed how many habits and minor addictions you have? Coffee, cigarettes, maybe certain kinds of foods and preferred times of day for eating. Your own way of hanging your clothes and organizing your refrigerator. You may be addicted to television news or a morning newspaper. You may be addicted to exercise or hot baths or lying in the sun.

Almost all of these habits have been developed over years and years through repetition. Men are particularly susceptible to repetition. They like rituals and the security of knowing everything will be the same.

You may have always thought that men want something new and different and exciting all the time. Not true. When it comes to a lifelong relationship, what they really want is security and happy, predictable regularity. In order to become a habit with a man, you will want to bring a little repetition into your relationship.

That means you should begin to plan your dates for certain nights of the week—every Saturday and Wednesday night, for example. He will develop the habit of seeing you then. If you miss one night, he'll find his habit interrupted and then he'll be yearning for you.

Through repetition, you can make your happy anchors and sexual anchors a habit with a man, associated with the sound of your voice, or just having you around.

Repetition doesn't come at the beginning of your relationship. It comes at a time when you're nearly ready to make a commitment with someone.

As a matter of fact, one way to tell if your love affair is ready to progress to something more involved is whether or not there is a regularity to the amount of time you spend together. Men seldom marry the girl they see irregularly. Usually it's the steadily growing love relationships that lead to marriage.

Our Song

Notice how some couples play the same music over and over again. It's "our song" they're playing. They can stand listening to it so many times because it is their personal "love experience trigger." For them, it is highly pleasurable. Through this addictive repetition, the song and the experience both become habitual parts of their lives.

Any mutually shared love trigger that is habit forming can add to a relationship. It doesn't have to be a song. Some couples have a silly little saying that only has meaning for them, or pet jokes that really aren't funny to anyone else, or private names they call each other. Repeating these makes their love a habit.

Some couples say the magic words, "I love you," a lot more than others. This verbal repetition gives these couples a better chance of becoming a habit with each other. You, of course, will be able to say the magic words in his particular Love Language.

To the visual man, you could say, "You can see how much I love you." To the auditory man, you might say, "You can hear how much I love you." To the feelings man, "You can feel how much I love you."

Praise

You've heard the old advice that the way to win a man is to praise him—that men can't get enough flattery. Truthfully, he likes the flattery, but what he really likes is the constant repetition of the loving feeling he gets from being flattered.

Flattery doesn't have to be vacuous or fawning. With a little loving thoughtfulness, it can come naturally and steadily, as you get to know each other better. For example, "Hey, that's yummy salad dressing. I like your brand better than mine." Or, "That's a clever way you've arranged your shoes. I never would have thought of that." Or, "You know what you said yesterday about————? Well, you were right."

One way your Mr. Right will become addicted to you is through the repetition of all the little pleasant habits and feelings he will associate with you. This will give him a feeling of stability and emotional security he doesn't get anywhere else in the world. Naturally, he'll feel driven to come back to you time and time again.

Your man will become dependent on the regularity of the love he receives. Like a drug addict, he will know there is predictable, repeated pleasure in being with you.

Handling Love's Problems

15

YOU'VE FOUND YOUR MR. RIGHT. YOU'VE FOLlowed The Love Plan and he fits right into your life. He's perfect. You're in love and you think he is too. Unfortunately, love is so hard to be sure of. The minute we find it we get scared. We're afraid that the love we've worked so hard for will disappear before it gets a chance to be nurtured and grow.

Fear of loss is one of the biggest problems you'll have to fight. It seems as though once you've begun to have a good relationship, you immediately start worrying about losing it. That's just human nature, but you must understand this reaction and control it.

The fear of losing your love can drive you to do terrible things to your relationship. It can make you jealous without reason. It can make you issue unrealistic ultimatums. It may lead you to destroy the relationship just as it's beginning to bloom into real love.

Controlling Fear of Loss

Many women suffer from typical fear-of-loss reactions the minute they find love. I can't tell you how many women have confessed to me, even after getting engaged to a wonderful man who loves her, "We're going to get married, if I live that long." Or, "I think I have cancer." Or, "Something's going to happen to me, I know it. I'm going to die before the wedding." Or, "Now that I've finally found him, I'm afraid something will happen to him. Every time he goes out I imagine someone calling to tell me there's been a terrible accident."

This kind of fear of success in love is as prevalent as fear of success in business. Many women will sabotage their own relationships because they are unconsciously afraid of succeeding. Success will mean a change of their whole lives. They won't be the deprived woman they've been for so long, the single struggling for success in a coupled world. Success in love involves some change in identity, and those who find love must be ready to accept that.

One way I found to overcome the fears that come with the beginning of love is through affirmations combined with exercise. The powerful physical and mental combination can exorcise even the most stubborn uncertainties.

Susanne and Jeffrey had been dating six months when he told her he loved her. Susanne's past relationships had been one broken heart after another until she met Jeff and their love started to blossom. Susanne then had a fear-of-success crisis because, deep down, she didn't really believe she deserved the love she had found.

She was feeling insecure and unhappy in spite of the fact that Jeff told her over and over that he loved her. "I can't believe he really loves me," she confessed. "And worse yet, after all these months of waiting for him to say it, I don't know how to respond. I tell him I love him, but I miss the crazy love feelings I've had in the past.

"Jeff and I have such a sane love that I'm worried. He doesn't go out with other women. I don't feel jealous. It's terrible, but without the insanity, I don't really feel like I'm in love."

Susanne was on the verge of blowing the first real love she ever had because she was too insecure to believe she deserved it. She had old programming that needed to be erased immediately. She thought that only a crazy "in love" feeling was valid. That her sane love with Jeff wasn't real.

Susanne also thought she wasn't pretty enough to be loved. She couldn't get the idea out of her mind until she began jogging and doing affirmations at the same time.

Exercise and Affirmations

Instead of counting steps, or singing or listening to the radio while she jogged, Susanne used her time to change her old programming. As she ran she repeated over and over again: "I am beautiful." "I am lovable." "I love Jeff." "Jeff loves me."

Every morning she said her affirmations, repeating them like a mantra, over and over, sometimes hundreds of times during her morning run. After just one week, Susanne began to feel better about her relationship with Jeff. She began to accept his love and return it without feeling as if she really didn't deserve it at all. She began to glow in her new security. She soon erased the old programming that said she didn't deserve the love she'd found.

If you find yourself suffering from fear of love, learn to erase the bad programming. Don't listen to the little nagging voice that says, "Maybe he really doesn't love me." Or, "Maybe he's got someone else on the side." Or, "I'm not pretty enough to keep him." Or, "I'm probably dying of a rare disease."

Instead, erase the old messages by replacing them with new, positive affirmations, as Susanne did. Call it brainwashing yourself if you like, but you'll be happier without those old messages telling you happiness is something you don't deserve.

Mirroring His Ideas

In Chapter Ten, we discussed different forms of mirroring as a way to get close to your man and win him. Mirroring can also help your communications once love begins to happen.

Mirroring what your man has just said by echoing his words isn't a good idea. But rephrasing what he just said, either to make sure you understood, or because you hope you misunderstood, can be a good idea.

You may find out you didn't understand what he meant at all or he may realize what he said didn't come out the way he meant it to. Mirroring his ideas is a good way to check things out, to make sure you're not jumping to conclusions.

Jumping to conclusions without checking things out is very destructive to a relationship. For example, he tells you he has to work late every night for a while. You immediately assume that means you won't be seeing each other. Better check it out. You could be wrong.

Sam and Fiona had a problem with their relationship for a long time. He was always saying things that hurt her or caused her to jump to conclusions. When she told me about his latest declaration she had worked herself up to a state of near hysteria.

Sam, thirty-six years old, held a middle-management position at a bank in Minneapolis and had a passion for scuba diving. He told Fiona one night over dinner, "I've always wanted to be near an ocean. Lake diving is okay, but I dream about ocean reefs, deep diving in clear, warm ocean water. Since I can't find that around here, I'm thinking about spending a couple of years in Hawaii, living right next to the ocean."

Fiona immediately assumed that meant life was over for her and Sam. She was crushed until she checked out what he was saying by mirroring his ideas. The next time she got a chance to talk to Sam (an auditory lover) she said, "I can hear that what you're doing now is a real clash with scuba diving and that you'd love to be near an ocean. Does that mean you'd be giving up your job and moving away to Hawaii to live?" she asked timidly, almost afraid to hear what he would answer.

"Maybe in twenty years," Sam told her, still oblivious to Fiona's reactions. "I could take early retirement and do what I've always wanted. Isn't that fun to think about?"

Fiona felt a little silly for being so upset, but she learned to check things out by mirroring his ideas immediately instead of letting things go for days at a time while she was upset.

What He Doesn't Say

Another way of checking things out is to find out the things he doesn't say. Be on the lookout for certain vague words in his conversation (words like "it," "that," "everything," "nothing," "them," "things"). If you stop and find out what he means exactly, you can save yourself a lot of grief.

How many times has a man gotten depressed and said, "Everything's turning to shit." Those are the times you have to ask the "What" question. Before you take him literally and decide you're part of "everything," ask him, "What exactly is going wrong?"

Or he says, "Some things just don't work out," and you're not sure of the context. Instead of assuming he's talking about your relationship, ask, "What things don't work out?"

Or he may say, "I'm really upset." Don't immediately assume he's upset about something you have or haven't done, or even something you have any control over. Find out first. Ask, "What exactly are you upset about?"

Other Women

Clara, a thirty-two-year-old unmarried secretary, decided to do everything right in her new relationship with Joe, a divorced father of two boys. "I made everything so terrific for Joe at my house, he never went home," she told me.

"At first, I thought all that was wonderful, but then I began to wonder whether it was right for him to be here all the time. The neighbors were beginning to ask questions like, 'Did you get married, dear?' so I suggested that we have a little time apart.

"Joe was a little hurt, but quick to pack his toothbrush and take off. It wasn't five minutes after he left that I began to miss him desperately. I couldn't wait the twenty minutes while he drove from my house to his so I could call him, and at least hear his voice on the phone.

"He didn't go right home. Instead he went to a bar for a few drinks. It was two hours before he got home. Meanwhile, of course, I was calling him constantly. It was crazy, but I was worried the whole time that he had gone right to another woman's house. I was sick with jealousy and fear.

"When I finally got him on the phone, he promised to come back right away. Then I felt really ridiculous."

What Clara hadn't counted on was that once you start making a love affair a habit, you can get addicted as easily as the man can. If that happens, a sudden jolt of jealousy can knock you off your feet.

As we discussed in the last chapter, love's addictive qualities can bring you closer together as a couple and lead to increasing commitment. The better your relationship is, the more addicted you both become to it. Unfortunately, the more addicted you are, the more you fear losing the source of your pleasure. Jealousy is fear of loss at its worst.

No one is immune to the "green-eyed monster." I have seen macho swingers throw up because their wife was doing "it" with someone else, even when they'd agreed before hand to experiment. I've comforted countless weeping women whose loved ones were "exploring" with someone younger, prettier, sexier, or just different. And I've had terrible attacks of jealousy myself.

In a world where we have been promised we can have it all—commitment and freedom to explore other relationships, security and love, spontaneity and truth—there is a seething rage because jealousy and hate, anger and disappointment are often products of the search for a perfect relationship. In the midst of what is supposed to be love, we are sometimes gripped by a wrenching pain.

Your Jealousy

Jealousy and envy are different. Jealousy in a love affair usually means you wish your partner would stop doing something he's doing—like seeing someone else. Envy is when you wish you were doing it too.

You will have no trouble telling the difference. Jealousy tears at your gut in exactly the same place you feel attached to the person you love.

Jealousy hits you suddenly, when he makes it obvious to someone on the phone that he can't really talk while you're there. Or when he breaks a date, or you find a slip of paper with a woman's name and phone number.

Jealousy happens when you find another woman's hairbrush, and you don't believe him when he says it's his daughter's. It's when he flirts just a little too long with another woman.

You suspect a lie, an infidelity, and you are driven to know who she is. What does she look like? Where did they go together? What do they do? Does he love her? Does she love him? Your brain is racked with jealous concerns. You hate yourself for having such tacky feelings.

Jealousy can drive you to do awful things to your relationship. You search his trash, looking for love letters from other women. You check his wallet, his briefcase, his appointment book. And you feel incredibly stupid, sneaky and scuzzy for doing it, but you just can't stop. We've all been there. But there are things you can do to help yourself.

First Aid for Jealousy

1. Admit your jealousy—if not to him, to yourself and a close friend. Remember, there's nothing to be ashamed of. If your relationship is supposed to be exclusive, or you've been seeing no one else, be upfront enough to tell the man in your life, "I'm hurt. I felt jealous." Don't be accusatory; just say how you feel. And don't be mealymouthed with euphemisms like, "I don't feel comfortable." *Never* lower yourself to asking about the other woman: "Is she pretty? Is she tall? Is she sexier than me?" Just because you feel jealous doesn't mean you have to get competitive. Never confront the other woman to try to get rid of her. It just won't work.

2. Which brings up *you.* Are you letting your own insecurity place unreasonable demands for fidelity on your lover? We all have our little insecurities, but you can't expect your lover to be your shrink. These days, monogamy develops slowly, as the relationship develops. Are you being realistic about your expectations? You wouldn't want someone that no one else wants, would you?

3. Until your relationship has matured into stable, committed exclusivity, self-esteem is your only defense against jealousy. Realize that there's only one of you in the world, that you are special, and that he has to want you and the special things you have to offer. If you're a short brunette and you find out your lover is dating a tall blonde, don't get upset. She's probably just as worried about his attraction to you as you are about her. In the long run, he'll choose you because you know so much more about how to reach his inner self. Just be patient.

4. Remember, jealousy comes from wanting to *own* another person. It is really the experience of having lost, or might lose. You really can't *own* a man, no matter how much you'd like to.

5. Be careful of the "reverse effect." Jealousy can make you go after a man who isn't at all right for you. He may not fit any of your requirements, and maybe you're only lukewarm about him. But the minute you find out he's dating two other women who are both crazy about him, he seems more interesting. The reason is that you are buoying up your own self-esteem by assuring yourself you are chasing a very desirable man. Winning him may seem more valuable because other women want him. Don't let jealousy twist your judgment. A good man is a good man, even if you're lucky enough to be the only one interested in him.

6. Continuing jealousy could be a sign that the relationship is in danger. Just as there is justifiable paranoia, so there is such a thing as appropriate jealousy. If your love relationship is actually in danger, your jealousy is a normal, appropriate reaction. If things don't change, you may have to find someone else.

His Jealousy

There's a fine line between a man who is possessive and caring for you, and a man who is out of control with jealousy. The former is flattering, the latter is dangerous. Jealous men have been known to beat up women. They are dangerous to others as well.

Gail, a twenty-six-year-old beautician, was going with Paul, an extremely jealous man. She was secretly flattered. "I know it isn't a healthy situation," she confessed, "but I love it when he thinks every man is after me. Actually, it only makes him want me more because he thinks I'm such a prize."

Then one night, Paul, a physical education teacher at a local high school, broke her door down in a fit of jealousy. He attacked a piano tuner who was fixing her piano. Gail begged him to stop. The neighbors called the police. Paul was arrested, the piano tuner wound up in the hospital, and Gail was evicted.

"I tried to reassure him all the time," she said, "but he never really believed I was faithful, no matter what I said."

Reassuring a jealous lover is exactly the wrong

thing to do. Resisting his jealousy, or trying to talk him out of it or coddle him out of it, will only make it worse. The longer you feed it, the longer the jealousy will continue.

If you are involved with a jealous lover, forget trying to keep his jealousy under control. Forget trying to build his self-esteem or assure him of your love. Don't always be patient and available. Don't tell him you'll be there forever. He won't believe you anyway.

Realize you are getting something out of the relationship that keeps you involved. If you want to continue getting the benefits of the relationship, you will have to learn to deal with his jealousy. Here are some rules.

1. Don't lie. If you get caught looking, or thinking, say, "Yes, I thought about it, but here's where I am."
2. Don't treat him with loving kindness when he's jealous. That just teaches him that acting jealous gets him love.
3. Don't put his feelings down. Talk about them with respect, but assure him you don't like his actions.
4. If reassuring him of your fidelity doesn't help, stop trying. It's evident that what he needs is therapy, not promises of perpetual fidelity.

Preventing Jealousy

Experts in the field of jealousy agree that jealousy feels just as bad whether it's rational or delusional, and that absolute truth between people is the only real preventive action that works.

If you're in a relationship that you believe has a real future, you'd do best to have a frank talk about exclusivity and jealousy—how you feel about dating other men and how you feel about him dating other women. You may decide you're ready to give up all others. If not, arrive at some understandings or ground rules, such as the following:

1. Consider outside sex and flirtations without emotional involvement and agree ahead of time whether it's okay or not.
2. Consider outside relationships with strangers only, or only out of town, or just when it's someone you don't love.
3. Consider one free night per week.
4. Consider sharing generalities, or specifics, on outside sex, or consider not sharing any information. But agree between you on how you will deal with information about a real or imagined indiscretion if it pops up.
5. If you want to do something that isn't in your ground rules and that might trigger jealousy, talk about it first, not afterward.
6. Make trust and honesty your first goal.

Why We Get Jealous

Some psychologists claim jealousy is instinctive, a trait inherited from our animal ancestors. Darwin, in his *Descent of Man*, observed jealousy in animals and linked it to human jealousy.

Other experts have accepted the Freudian theory that jealousy, instilled by loss of mother, is inevitable. Freud said, "Jealousy is one of those affective states like grief, that may be described as normal. If anyone appears to be without it, the inference is justified that it has undergone severe repression and consequently plays all the greater part in his unconscious mental life."

Perhaps, if the renowned philosophers and psychologists are right about jealousy, the best coping device for jealousy in ourselves and others is compassion.

Don't Fight

16

NATURALLY, ANY RELATIONSHIP HAS CONFLICTS. But there are ways to solve those conflicts without fighting. Whatever you do, don't fight with a man unless you are fighting for something really important and there is absolutely no other way to solve the problem.

Sure, there are those few couples for whom fighting seems to be a way of life, but for most people, fighting is destructive to a relationship. The newest theories about anger go counter to the old theories of "getting it out." Now, psychologists believe that anger expressed only creates more anger.

Fighting may clear the air in a relationship and it may make the participants feel better afterward when they make up, but it's a strain that you don't need. Neither does he.

If the man in your life finds that he's always angry because of frequent fighting, he may well have second thoughts about the future of the relationship. Fighting can quickly drive a man away. He thinks to himself, "Am I going to spend the rest of my life fighting with this woman? Hell, no. I'm going to get out before I'm stuck."

You may feel you have always been justified in every fight you've had with a man. But that's not really the point. Unfortunately, what counts is your man's perception of you. No man wants to spend the rest of his life with a harridan.

Even if your relationship survives fighting, there will be scars. When you're fighting, you're both liable to say something that will permanently damage your relationship. Basically, the trouble with fighting with a man is that you are the one who is likely to get hurt—directly or indirectly.

Not fighting, however, doesn't mean that you should give in all the time and just let him have his own way. Self-esteem is very important in your love life—for both parties.

How many times have you heard the statement, "If you can't love yourself, you can't love someone else." If you make too many compromises for your loved one, you are going to start feeling bad about yourself. You'll begin to resent him for making you change what you really want, and you'll hate yourself for doing things you're not proud of.

So if you've found yourself giving in all the time, or fighting all the time, or faced with having to choose between the two, you might want to change your approach.

There are ways for you to stand up for yourself, ask for what you want, and get what you want in your love relationship—without doing battle.

Reflecting

A special form of mirroring, reflecting your lover's behavior verbally, will often get him to slow down and look at things from your point of view.

Jon, who was very much a feelings lover, was always shouting at Linda until she learned to reflect his behavior, not by shouting back at him, but by simply saying, "I wonder why you feel you have to shout at me."

She had simply mirrored his behavior for him in a verbal way. If he had been an auditory man she could have said, "It sounds like you think you have to shout at me." If he was visual, she could say, "It looks like you think you have to shout at me."

Let's say your lover is in a rotten mood. He's been taking it out on you. You say to the feelings lover, "I understand how angry you are." To the hearing lover, "I hear how angry you are." To the visual lover, "I can see how angry you are."

He immediately feels better. It's the same principle that a doctor uses. Ever notice that the minute she says, "I can understand why you feel so awful," you feel better. It's because she has made you feel justified, not defensive or angry. You have started with an agreement about your condition, and so you just naturally feel better about taking orders. The same holds true for a man. Once you agree with his feelings (not meaning that you think his feelings are justified, just that you understand he has them), then he can listen to you better. Try it. You'll be amazed at the results.

Let's say he's complaining that you haven't been sexually aggressive lately. He says he always has to make all the moves. But he really seems mad, ready to make a fight over this. Instead of defending yourself, or giving excuses, or attacking him by telling him all his shortcomings in bed, try reflecting his feelings.

To a visual man say, "It looks like you feel unloved because I haven't been aggressive enough lately." To an auditory man, "It sounds like you feel unloved because . . . ," and to the feelings man, "I sense that you feel unloved. . . ."

You'll be amazed how close this technique will bring you, even in the middle of an argument. The reason is that suddenly you are no longer disagreeing with him. Maybe you're even on his side.

He'll stop fighting at this point. After all, it's virtually impossible to continue fighting with someone who appears to be agreeing with you. But what do you do next?

Venting

If you've been following The Love Plan, you probably know your lover better than he knows himself. But if you haven't, it's just possible that your lover has a long list of grievances he's carrying around inside his head. What he starts a fight over may be the least important of the things that are bothering him. Try to get his whole grievance list out in the open. Then you can deal with it.

Taking the last example, you would be wise to ask, "What exactly makes you feel that I haven't been aggressive enough?"

He might reply, "Well, for one thing, you haven't gone down on me in two weeks!"

Instead of arguing the point or putting him down with a caustic comment about his "oral sex diary," stay cool. You're on a roll here, finding out some things about your man that you really need to know. Follow up, saying, "Gee, maybe I haven't. What else makes you feel that way?"

After hearing that he doesn't really have any other specific complaints in the sex department, you might go on and say, "I can tell that you're still angry. Is there something else that makes you feel unloved?"

There may be. He might say, "Yeah. Whenever we go out to parties, you never stay with me, you spend the whole evening with your friends."

Soon, you'll have the full list of grievances, real or imagined, that may have been affecting the relationship for weeks or months. You'll also have a surprisingly calmed-down lover. Just having you listen to his feelings is a large part of what he wants.

Of course, you may have been unjustly accused on all counts, and we'll come to that. But right now what you need to do is quietly review the list with him. By reflecting back to him all of the complaints he has vented, you will convince him that you understand him. He will be in a completely conciliatory mood.

Now is the time to deal with the complaints, one

by one, and find out how strongly he feels about each. Once they've been vented and they're "on the table," you may find that the steam has gone out of most of them. He may concede he's wrong on some. For those that are potentially serious disagreements, at least they've been defined, and you will find that one or more of the following techniques will enable you to deal with them.

Self-Disclosure

Self-disclosure is a great way to get close, and to solve arguments as well. Revealing something about yourself, especially if it's the same as "his" revelation, can bring you closer.

Sam, a powerful oceanfront developer, and Debby, a real-estate saleswoman, were having a terrific love affair. They were able to do business together as well as make love. Everything was going well with them except for one thing. Her kids. He hated them, but he loved her.

Debby shared custody of her kids with her ex-husband. The kids had become more than a little spoiled by their wealthy father. The kids were so hard to live with, he gave them a house of their own, a maid and an allowance. They were independently arrogant—and almost uncontrollable whenever they came to stay with Debby.

But they were her flesh and blood, and she loved them. At first, Debby tearfully defended her kids whenever they did something wrong. But it was a losing cause. No sooner had she apologized because one of the boys broke Sam's window in his car, then another one of the kids spilled paint all over the floor. Sam couldn't stand them, didn't want to be around them, not for Christmas, or Easter, or birthdays, or anything.

Debby finally realized that there was no defense for her kids. They were a handful only a mother could love. One day she and Sam were into one of their typical fights. Sam had just bailed Debby's oldest out of jail for shoplifting. He was furious.

"Those kids are the worst kids I've ever been around. They should all be put in reform school," he shouted at Debby.

Instead of shouting back, arguing, or defending the kids, Debby used a combination of self-disclosure and mirroring (see Chapter Ten). "You're right! If they weren't my own, I'd put them away myself," she told him. "The truth is, sometimes I hate the little monsters myself. I've had days when I wish they'd just disappear."

Sam was shocked. "Now, now," he changed his tune. "Maybe we're being too hard on them." Because Debby had first gotten into a state of agreement with Sam (using self-disclosure), he became willing to soften his attitude—and maybe find a way to live with the problem.

Winning with Humor

Humor can be used to defuse any argument—if it's not bitter or accusing humor.

Sandra used humor to get over a problem with David. Sandra, an artist, was extremely messy, but very creative. David, an engineer, was very intelligent and also very neat. They had been dating for several months when the hostilities broke out.

David insisted that Sandra clean her apartment or, he said, he was never coming over there again. That meant that if Sandra wanted to see David, she had to be the one to drive all the way across town for their dates.

For a while, Sandra did the driving, but that wasn't enough. She wasn't just messy at home. She was messy at David's as well. They were fighting over her bad housekeeping all the time until Sandra learned to react to her own foibles with humor instead of anger.

If David said something about the mess in her car, she told him, "I just cleaned it up. You should have seen it yesterday." If he happened to see her apartment and it was in its usual shambles, she joked, "You caught me in the middle of housecleaning. Don't look."

Humor, used wisely, can reduce the tension inherent in any argument. It's almost impossible to stay mad when you're laughing.

"Broken Record"

What happens if, in spite of your best efforts, hostility breaks out? It starts over something small—like he never puts the toilet seat down, or you always put the garbage in the wrong bag. Soon you are both shouting at each other. What's the best way to fight—without escalating the fight?

Karla and Howard were a classic "odd couple." She wanted the alarm clock on her side of the bed. He wanted it on his. She wanted to eat late, he wanted to eat early. She liked fancy French food, he liked health food. She loved to go dancing, he liked to stay home.

For some reason Karla was deeply in love with Howard, in spite of the fact that he wanted to run her life.

Howard had a tendency to be critical and nag Karla. He'd nag her about her health and her way of life. "How can you sleep so late in the mornings? Don't you know it's bad for you?"

Howard not only insisted that Karla get up earlier, he was also a real bully about her eating habits. "You shouldn't eat that junk," he told her continually and, worse yet, he was always trying to force vitamins and health foods on her. "Eat this," he'd insist. "It's good for you," he'd tell her.

"I know what's good for me. I've managed to stay alive and be healthy for twenty-seven years. I don't need you to tell me what to do," Karla would shout back. Howard, a chiropractor, felt he had every right to tell her what to do.

"I'm a doctor," he'd insist. "I know about these things."

"You're not a real doctor," she'd shout at him.

Their fights just continued to escalate—until Karla learned other ways to stick to her guns without really fighting. She learned the "Broken Record" technique for winning a fight without getting upset.

To use the Broken Record technique to keep out of a fight, simply restate your opinion without getting angry. Karla, for instance, learned to deal with Howard without fighting by first reflecting his beliefs and then using the Broken Record technique. When he would try to bully her into eating something she didn't want, she'd say, "Howard, I understand how you might feel the way you do, but I'm going to eat what I've always eaten."

At first Howard would shout back at her, "That's dumb. How could you eat poison?" And she'd simply answer with the Broken Record technique, saying the same sentence, "Howard, I can understand how you feel, but I'm going to eat what I've always eaten."

In the beginning, Karla reported, she must have repeated herself ten or twenty times. Instead of arguing back as she had in the past, she just calmly repeated her position. Howard was dumbfounded, but Karla stuck to her guns.

Karla found she was the one who remained mellow and relaxed in the face of Howard's upset. Soon, there was no fight left in Howard because he had no one left to fight with. He learned that he couldn't get her into an argument and he gave up trying to browbeat and argue her into doing what he wanted.

Had Howard been a visual lover instead of a feelings one, Karla could have said, "I can see why you feel that way, but I'm going to continue to eat the way I want." If he'd been a hearing type, Karla could have told Howard, "I can hear what you're saying, but I intend to continue to eat what I want."

What happened is that when Howard criticized Karla, he expected her to fight back. When she didn't, he had to admit that his approach simply wasn't working. Karla also learned another way of dealing with Howard's domineering tendencies.

Agreement

Agreement is a technique that is nicely complementary with the Broken Record technique. By agreeing that Howard might be right but that she was still unwilling to change, Karla found a new way of sticking to her original desires. She also learned to let Howard vent his anger once in a while, since that seemed to be such an important part of his personality.

She would say to Howard, "Yes, you're right, I'm a terrible eater." She was asserting her right to have her alleged negative quality, to be herself.

By agreeing with Howard's criticisms and yet asserting her right to continue with whatever behavior he didn't like, Karla was able to say, "I am me," and "I have a right to be the way I am," without getting into a huge argument.

She was telling Howard in a subtle way, "I have the right to be who I am, and you have the right to leave me if you don't like it." But simultaneously, Karla was offering an olive branch, by sympathizing with him for living with such an unhealthy person.

She would occasionally allow him to tell her everything that was wrong with the way she ate, just to get it off his chest. She still wasn't arguing back with him or getting into a fight, she was simply allowing him to vent his feelings.

These techniques for avoiding fights do not mean that you give up your own beliefs or desires. They simply provide various ways to first get on the same wavelength as the man in your life. He then becomes nonbelligerent, much more likely to change his mind.

A man is much easier to persuade when you start

from a state of being in agreement with him—even if you're only in agreement on a negative point. Then you can get him to see things your way.

But what if you've avoided the argument, you're both looking at the conflict, and you still disagree? There are honest differences of opinion between any two people, and they are bound to occur, sooner or later, in a relationship.

Negotiating

What do you do if you hit an impasse? You and your lover both think you're being calm and reasonable, yet you still disagree. He says he expects his number one female companion to enjoy things he likes, to spend time going to sporting events, which you hate. You say you expect your number one man to go to concerts and ballet performances, which he hates.

You have three possibilities to negotiate the situation. One possibility is you both find someone else to go to those events with. Another is for you to trade off—you go with him, then he goes with you. The third possibility is to negotiate a solution involving other aspects of your daily lives.

For instance, you think he should do more repairs around your apartment. If he fixes three things, you go to the football game. He thinks you should help him organize his files. You organize one file drawer, he goes to the ballet.

Negotiating in relationships doesn't have to be in black and white. In other words, just because you want different things doesn't mean somebody has to lose. You can win by setting up the same kind of win–win negotiation for your relationship as you would in business. Make it so that you both win.

You cook him dinner, he goes to the ballet. He fixes your faucet, you go to the football game. You have both gotten something you want. There are no losers.

The first step to negotiating or making a contract with your lover about something is to change your negative complaints into positive requests. Don't tell him, "I don't want you to look at other women when we're out." Instead say, "I'd like you to pay more attention to me when we're together."

Don't say, "I don't want to go to any more Italian restaurants." Instead say, "I'd like to go to another type of restaurant besides Italian."

The reason you have to change your negative complaints to positive requests is twofold. One, men react negatively to complaints. In other words, he'll think you're just whining. The second reason is that once you have changed from negative complaints to positive requests, you have something to negotiate.

Find out *his* complaints. Change them to positive requests. For instance, he says, "You never cook for me." What he really means is "I'd like you to cook for me sometimes." He says, "You don't act aggressive enough." He means, "I'd like you to be aggressive more often."

Once you have changed his complaints to positive requests, you can negotiate with him, agreeing to do certain things he wants in return for his doing certain things you want. For example, "I'll cook your favorite dinner once a week if you'll agree to leave the toilet seat down." Or, "I'll be more aggressive if you'll take the trash out."

These are the kinds of negotiations that can turn out positively, because you both have something to gain. Make sure you always offer a win–win negotiation to the man in your life. It's irresistible.

In some unfortunate circumstances, none of the above techniques will work. He won't stop fighting because he's pathologically incapable. You can't negotiate because neither of you is willing to compromise. Then you have to find someone else. Fighting as a way of life doesn't improve, it only gets worse.

If you're stuck in a relationship with a man who is incompatible, who wants to fight and is unwilling to negotiate or compromise, you need to rethink your Love Plan. You may have chosen the wrong man. The only smart thing to do is find someone else who is willing to work things out.

Relationships require working out. The fact that you're reading a book on how to make a man fall in love with you shows you are willing to work to get a relationship right.

You deserve a man who is willing to work with you. Go back to Chapter Three, start over by taking your Man Plan seriously, then follow The Love Plan exactly. You and your True Love will soon be ready for the next powerful love technique—spell casting.

Casting a Spell

17

"I'LL NEVER FORGET THE WAY HE LOOKED AT her," my heartbroken friend Carol told me after accidentally running into her ex and his new love at a party. "His eyes were glazed over, he had a stupid grin on his face, and he hung on her every word with what seemed like absolute rapture.

"If I didn't know him better, I'd swear he was on drugs or something. He seemed to be experiencing an altered state of consciousness. He almost had a dazed expression. I tried to look pleasant but I was suffering inside. I didn't want him to be so happy without me.

"He thought her every sneeze was a new delight. It made me sick with jealousy. He obviously needed a deprogrammer just to think of anything but her.

"He hardly noticed me or anyone else all night long. He couldn't take his eyes off her. He was mesmerized, and I was crushed. I went home and cried all night. I just couldn't forget the expression on his face when he looked at her."

My friend Carol was upset because she had never been able to create that kind of feeling in a man she loved. "He never looked at *me* that way," she cried. "I want a man to look at me with that much love. I don't understand it. I'm prettier than she is and I'm smarter, yet I can tell she's got him under her spell in a way I never did. How does she do it?"

You've probably known women with a lot less on the ball than you who always have men falling all over themselves in love with them. Maybe they have lumpier figures, six kids from a previous marriage, and messy houses, yet men constantly find them irresistible.

You've already learned that part of their secret is that these women have an instinctive ability to get on a man's wavelength. Intuitively, they sense his Love Language. But there's more. They automatically mirror him and develop a sense of trust and love in him. That is the starting point for weaving a spell.

Building a sense of trust with a man is very important. When he is very small, a man develops an image of an all-forgiving, all-loving female figure—his mother. She's the one who takes him in her arms and makes everything okay, who solves all his problems, no matter what they are.

Every man is hesitant to trust a woman other than his mother. Often he has had bad experiences with other relationships. He is resistant to loving and giving because he is afraid he'll get hurt. With a few powerful new techniques that build on those you've already learned, you can overcome his resistance to new ideas, to you, and to love.

At this point in The Love Plan, you are now like a ballet dancer who has learned all the positions and the proper execution of the basic steps. Now it is time to put those steps together into a dance.

You know the techniques for communicating with a man in his Love Language, for fostering intimacy by mirroring him and anchoring his good feelings. By now you should know your lover better than you've ever known any man. You know how to get what you want in bed, and how much to give in the relationship. Your man is like putty in your hands. More important, he is falling in love with you.

Now, if you're *sure* that you want this love affair to grow into a truly committed relationship, The Love Plan will show you how. You will learn to weave a magic spell around the man you love that will always make him want to say yes to you.

For anyone who has followed The Love Plan diligently, casting a spell is only a small step beyond the techniques you already know—and it's easy. So easy, in fact, that you should stop for a moment, reassess the situation, and be sure that you are really ready to go forward.

Don't Use It Unless You're Sure

Up to here, the techniques of The Love Plan can be used to explore a man, to find out if he's right for you, and to create a wonderful love affair. If, for any reason, you have misgivings about deepening the relationship further, don't start weaving a spell. Not with this man.

If you were to break up now, you both would feel the normal pain of ending a relationship, but your man won't be totally devastated. He'll have happy memories, and it's likely you'll remain good friends. But if you weave your spell to make him go along with your relationship objectives, you assume a real responsibility.

If you use The Love Plan to make a man commit himself to you, you should also be prepared to commit yourself to him. If you want him to give his all, you should be ready to do the same.

Weaving a spell is a powerful tool. It can help you "land" the man of your dreams, or it can break his heart. Use it responsibly.

That Old Black Magic

Weaving a seductive spell, creating a slightly altered state or consciousness, is one of the oldest and most effective love techniques in the world. Tokyo Rose used it on American GIs in World War II when she lulled them into listening. Mata Hari used it to learn military secrets. Cleopatra did it to Anthony and Caesar. Now you can do it too.

What makes a man fall totally in love? What does he say the experience is? "She makes me happy."

She *makes* him happy. That's the final clue to making a man fall in love with you. She "makes" him feel somehow different than he does at any other time—warm, relaxed, loving and agreeable.

What we're now discussing goes beyond close

communication. The fact that he can't really understand or account for all of this is precisely the point. The woman he loves has *woven a mysterious spell around him.*

She is his geisha, his Scheherazade, his Mata Hari all rolled up in one. Her spell is far more powerful than her looks or personality. How does she do it? Up to now, by being one of the few women who has the inborn, intuitive ability. What does she do? She tells stories that just happen to come to her, without really understanding how or why the stories cast a magic spell.

Now, you can cast the same spells just as easily, because you'll know exactly what stories to tell and exactly how to tell them. And you'll have the advantage of understanding exactly *why* the story induces a state of trust and relaxation, of acceptance and agreement.

Scheherazade told stories that saved her life. Your job is a little easier. You already have a man falling in love with you. Your stories can be simpler, designed to get your man to agree with you on something, to make changes in himself or your relationship—and to like making those changes.

Set the Stage

Set the stage first. If you're at all into cooking, especially if you've cooked for him before, cook something nice tonight. Mothers are right—the smell of good things cooking *does* make a man feel relaxed (it's primal, instinctive—don't fight it now).

Wear something you're sure he likes—sexy but not screamingly seductive. Most important, try to mirror what you think he'll wear. Burn his favorite incense and put on his favorite perfume. You want all his senses feeling relaxed and receptive. Light a fire in the fireplace. If you don't have a fireplace or it's summer, some candles are a good substitute. When he comes over, your place will be almost womblike in its warmth, good feelings—and safety.

Be sure to have music on. Choose something that approximates sixty beats per minute—the most relaxing tempo because it simulates the human heartbeat and makes people more receptive to new information.

Experts in the Bulgarian art of superlearning suggest that the best music for this purpose is the slow movements of the baroque composers—Bach, Handel, Vivaldi, Corelli, Telemann, and Pachelbel. If you are unfamiliar with them, try *The Four Seasons* by Vivaldi, Handel's *The Water Music,* Corelli's *Concerti Grossi Opus,* numbers 3,5,8, and 9, and Pachelbel's *Canon in D.*

If your lover prefers a more contemporary sound, try the music of Steve Halpern, Georgia Kelly, Paul Horn, or the Environments series.

In getting ready for your man, don't do a lot of things you've never done before, because he'll feel "set up." But by now in your love affair, you've probably done each one of these "stage-setting" things before. Tonight, you orchestrate them all together, and into this seductive heaven comes an uptight man, filled with his own problems. That's when you begin to cast your spell.

Getting Him to Say Yes

You're ready and confident. You've already learned, long before tonight, how to get your man into a relaxed, agreeable state. In your conversation over dinner, be attentive to him, but remember to touch on enough memory triggers and anchors to assure a romantic mood.

After dinner, relax together. Snuggle with him in a way that allows you both to watch him and touch him. You will be watching him closely to be sure he is fully relaxed and receptive. Then, use a good feelings anchor as you talk. While you're talking, sit as he sits, breathe as he breathes, and try to time your speech to his breathing. Break your phrases when he takes a breath.

The spell consists of four statements. The first three are simple statements that are obviously true, with which he can be in immediate, comfortable agreement. The fourth is what you want him to agree with.

Modulate your voice and talk slowly. Give him time to accept the first three ideas and verify their truthfulness in his own experience. The first two statements should be phrased in his Love Language. The next should be in a different language.

For the last statement, the point you want him to agree with, switch back to his language.

For example, let's say he's always seemed reluctant to make long-range plans with you. Let's also say his Love Language is visual. You are sitting together on the couch in front of the fireplace.

You touch his good feelings anchor and say, "Seeing us here together (the first agreement in his visual Love Language), watching the fire (the second visual agreement), and listening to the music (the third agreement, switching to an auditory Love Language), makes me see a wonderful future for us.

(You now return to his visual Love Language.) Can't you picture how nice it would be to take our vacation together this summer?" you ask—and he can't refuse. You have just cast your first spell.

It's deceptively simple. On a superficial level, it appears that you have told him a little story, the first part of which is so unarguably true and pleasant that he is seduced into going along with your ending. But there's more to it than that. On a psychological level, the "simple little story" is actually very carefully framed and constructed.

The mirroring and anchoring put him in a trusting and receptive mood. Your first two statements, in his Love Language, crystallized this mood into one of willing agreement. Your third statement was equally true—but was a subtle digression into another Love Language. Subconsciously, he was momentarily disoriented, anxious for you to return to his Love Language. When you did, he embraced *what* you were saying right along with the language shift. Subtle, but psychologically true and very powerful.

You don't have to have the inborn talent of a Scheherazade. The Love Plan has brought you, step by step, to this point, and you're on firm, familiar ground. You know your man and love him. Further, you're not trying to induce him to do something illegal or contrary to his deep beliefs. You can cast a spell to get what you want—partly because you now know the psychological techniques—and partly because what you want is probably pretty close to what he wants (except he doesn't know it yet).

Men are particularly receptive to a spell because so many of them are unable to express how they are feeling at any time, even though their feelings are bursting inside them. In essence, you are mirroring his unspoken (perhaps unacknowledged) feelings—acting as a biofeedback instrument for him.

You should know, if you are in tune with your man, that there is some part of him that wants what you want. (If not, you shouldn't be asking for it.) When you cast a spell, you bring that part of him to the surface.

Deep down, every man has a fantasy woman—an exciting seductress who will take him where he's never been—and with whom his heart is safe. As you cast your spells over your man, you will become this fantasy woman. And he will fall hopelessly in love with you.

The Love Plan includes many variations and uses of the techniques of spell casting. One of these variations is the "seductive story."

Seductive Stories

Have you ever wondered why some women are always being showered with gifts and taken away on exotic vacations? They often use seductive stories to get what they want. A seductive story is just a slightly different variation of casting a spell.

The seductive story telling technique is to stimulate your man's imagination about how wonderful it would be for him to do something you want. As a variation on the example I just gave you, let's assume that the issue is not his unwillingness to make future plans together, but, instead, his inertia. He's perfectly happy never going anywhere. You, on the other hand, want a vacation on a warm beach.

Don't just leave brochures lying around or whine

about how long it's been since you've been away. Instead, tell him a seductive story.

Always start your story in your man's Love Language. If he's visual, start out visual. Say, "You know, I keep getting this picture of us alone together on a desert island. We're watching the bright sun shining on the water, the waves rolling in. . . ." Then switch to feelings. ". . . and then I rub you all over with suntan oil, you get this giant erection and we make wild love all day. . . ." Then, back to the visual. "Afterward, we wake up and see the moonlight reflecting on the ocean."

If he's auditory, start by saying, "We'd listen to the surf gently lapping on the beach and get in tune with the sound of the tradewinds in the palm trees. . . ."

If your man is a feelings man, start by saying, "We'd feel the warm sun on our skin and the sand between our toes. . . ."

Little Spells to Solve Problems

As any relationship develops, there are inevitable differences to work out and hurdles to overcome. It is always better to resolve a problem than to hope it will go away.

Now that you understand the principles involved in casting a spell, you have an easy and effective way to deal with relationship problems as they occur. Instead of telling a story, you simply talk about the problem using some of the spell-casting techniques.

For example, you've dated a few months. You know he's in love with you and not seeing anyone else, but he hasn't yet told you he loves you. He's shy of making a love commitment. You've found out that his reticence is due to being hurt in relationships in the past.

You say, "You know, you're very wise not to make a commitment without really knowing the other person. We've both been in love with people before who turned out to be a big disappointment, and you're right not to rush into a relationship. It's nice that we've taken time to get to know each other so now we can be sure of our love."

Mirror his objections with three statements, and then "lead" him with one more statement that he will automatically want to accept as true because the ones before it have been so true. Remember to use his Love Language for the first two statements, another for the third, and then his own for the final statement you want him to agree with. Mirror his breathing, if you can. Break your thoughts in rhythm with his breaths.

For a feelings man: "We've both been hurt in the past . . . fallen for someone cold and unresponsive . . . but we can see how we've learned from our mistakes . . . and so we know we can trust each other . . . to make our love warm and secure . . . a real bond that grows between us."

You have started out by mirroring his objections along with his Love Language. The first three statements are not only true, they show your acceptance of his belief systems. Naturally, the last statement is not as verifiably true as the first three, but he will automatically tend to agree with the last.

You will, with practice, be able to make three agreement statements before bringing up what you want. You will have to think about it a little ahead of time, because each situation will demand its own impromptu script. With practice, it will only take you a minute or so to figure out your "script." You will be able to conjure up a little spell, on the spot, to solve problems that arise. Here's another example.

A woman who wanted her auditory lover to go to a party with all her old friends from college said to him:

"Bill, I can hear from the tone of your voice that the party sounds boring to you. You don't want to listen to a bunch of raucous strangers jabber about old times, or get trapped looking at some old yearbook, but you'll get to talk to some interesting business contacts there and we can come home and make beautiful music together afterward."

Because you start out agreeing with his objections, the first thing that happens is that he starts really listening to you—instead of thinking about how to argue his case. As soon as he hears his position validated, his unconscious feeling of resistance fades and is replaced with a feeling of agreement.

Secret Messages

Have you ever noticed how men seem to do the exact thing you ask them not to do?

You say, "Don't forget to stop on your way over and pick up some wine for dinner." Naturally he doesn't bring the wine.

It happens so often that you might think he's being obstinate. Or that he really doesn't want to do anything you say, or that he just doesn't listen. None of those things is true.

The truth is that he is listening, but his conscious mind sometimes misses the "don't" part of your message. All he hears is, "Forget to stop on your way home to pick up some wine for dinner."

The human mind has an unconscious tendency to ignore negative commands. Everything you've said registers—except for one little word, "don't," which gets filtered out. Of course, the omission of that one word completely reverses the overall message. If you're clever, you can learn to use this unconscious tendency to your advantage.

The principle of secret messages is the same one involved if I were to say to you, "Don't think about pink elephants." Naturally, the first thing that comes to your mind is pink elephants. Or if I said to you, "Don't think about pink sheep." You'd instantly have a whole flock of pink sheep in your mind.

The traditional forms of "Don't do" something, even "Please don't," are all unreliable. For example, you say to a man, "Please don't forget to make our reservations for dinner tonight." What does he hear? He hears, "Forget to make our reservations for dinner tonight."

The positive request is what's heard. So instead of telling your lover, "Don't forget to call me when you arrive," tell him, "Remember to call me when you arrive." Then he will. You should get into the habit of using positive, rather than negative, requests at all times with your lover. It will get your message across more reliably and generally improve communications between you. The Secret Message, though, goes one step further.

Advertisers use Secret Messages a lot. They understand the reverse advantage of negative messages. Advertisers know exactly what they're doing when they say, "Don't shop here first." They know you will. Or, "Don't buy our brand before you've tried the others." What you hear is the Secret Message, "Buy our brand before you've tried the others."

Let's say you're ready for your relationship to be exclusive. You think your lover really is, too, but he's still seeing other women occasionally out of habit or to assert his independence. It's a touchy issue, and you're not sure how to weave it into a spell.

Add Secret Messages to your spell. Say, "We both have enjoyed our independence, and we're used to going out with a lot of different people. You don't want to stop seeing other women, I know, but it is nice to know we can count on each other for the important things."

Of course, what will sink in very effectively is, "You . . . want to stop seeing other women."

A different kind of Secret Message is the imbedded question. Instead of asking your man, "How come your last marriage broke up?" for example, you would be better off using a secret question hidden in a statement. You could say instead, "I don't know anything about your last relationship."

As another example, you don't know if he plans to stay over. You might say, "We haven't discussed whether you'll be here for breakfast."

By couching your questions in a statement, you have softened their inquisitive edge. He will be more likely to answer you as well. Men are always nervous when women start asking direct questions. Ask yours with subtlety and you'll be surprised how much more responsive he is.

PARABLES

A parable is another way to get a man to change his mind without arguing. Ruth, a travel agent, had been going with Jack, a television director, for some months. Jack was getting close to making a real commitment to Ruth, but was still occasionally tempted by the young starlets he was always meeting. This naturally bothered Ruth, but she was wise enough not to issue any ultimatums. Instead, she used a clever parable to get Jack thinking about settling down.

She asked Jack, "If you were going to take a long airplane trip, say around the world, and you had your choice of going on a new sleek airplane that looked beautiful, but had never been tested or flown before, or going on a reliable plane like a 747, which would you feel safest on?"

It didn't take long for Jack to get the message. Without any arguing, Ruth made her point with Jack. Deep down underneath, he was ready to commit himself to Ruth and give up taking chances with the relationship.

If you have a sore subject you want to talk about with the man in your life, stop and think for a moment before you demand, argue, or nag. Pretend you're Scheherazade. Ask yourself what would she do to win her way and have her man love her all the more for it. All of her techniques are now at your disposal.

Weaving It All Together

As you grow more familiar with these techniques, seductive stories will come easier for you. It will begin to feel natural to cast a little spell over your man. It will be fun for you—and captivating for him.

The little stories and spells will begin to weave together, merging into an ongoing spell that he willingly steps into whenever he is with you. Don't ever worry that a man will resent your knowing his inner thoughts, seductively leading him to do new things. Have you ever seen a man "wrapped around a woman's finger" who didn't look deliriously happy?

It is truly every man's fantasy to have his own Scheherazade. He will find this magic with you and only you. Soon, the magic will make him want to be with you always.

When Love Happens

18

YOU'RE IN LOVE. HOW DO YOU KNOW? YOU HAVE all the signs. You feel lighter than air and you smile quietly whenever you think of him. You think of him all the time. You can't wait until you see or hear from him again. Nothing makes you happier than knowing you will see your beloved soon.

When you're apart, you imagine how it will be when you are together. You begin to think of having his children. You wonder about the practical problems of being together. Where would the two of you live? Would you marry first or just live together for a while?

You agonize over meeting his family, hoping, praying they will like you, and that you will like them. You imagine your wedding. You think about how he will ask you.

You spend most of your time talking about him to anyone who will listen. Naturally, you think he's more wonderful, more handsome, more intelligent, kinder, and cleverer than anyone you've ever met before. Even his qualities that someone else might see as (God forbid) negative somehow are cute and adorable to you. You love his stubborn streak and see it as admirable stick-to-itiveness. You even adore his obvious little weaknesses. You imagine you and him growing old together.

Nothing but him seems to matter so much. Not your job, not your lifelong goals, not your family, or friends. You're only happy if he is happy. If he's sad, or unresponsive, your day is ruined. It's embarrassing how you have put him first, ahead of almost everything.

You want to improve. Suddenly you are driven to lose those last few pounds, to be more attractive to him. You race to the gym, trying desperately to work off love's almost endless energy. The excitement of the chase has captured you. You are willing to compete, to go all out to win this man.

You know you can work out the problems any relationship has from time to time. You are willing to see through the normal testing period couples have before they learn to trust each other totally. You are committed to the goal of making a relationship work with him. You are willing to work to overcome problems and adversities. Sometimes the problems just make you more determined to see your love through—like Romeo and Juliet, the eternal starcrossed lovers, your yearning is just increased by obstacles.

Suddenly, all the other men you've ever known, even the new cute ones you meet, pale next to your loved one. Only he wears the magic halo that your love bestows. Suddenly you see why all the other men you've ever loved were wrong for you. There is only one true love and you have found him. Your goal in life is to be with him all the time, forever.

Clinching the Commitment

If you've followed The Love Plan without deviating and without resorting to the old tricks that don't work, you won't have to "make" him commit himself to you. He will want to.

Your man wants to have a secure and happy relationship as much as you do. When it comes time to ask you to marry him, he will ask. You will notice, of course, signs of growing commitment along the way.

He begins to date you every weekend.
You begin seeing each other during the week as well.
You find you are together on a regular schedule.
Your relationship is happy ninety percent of the time.
You begin to miss each other whenever you're apart.
He gives you little gifts.
You spend holidays together.
You meet his family and he meets yours.
You take vacations together.

He proposes (the nice old-fashioned way),
OR,
You start to live together.
You acquire property together.
You have open, relaxed discussions about the pros and cons of marriage.
You make lifelong commitments to each other.

Who Asks?

Each of the above steps in commitment can only happen if the man is a willing participant. You can find out about his willingness to make some commitments before he actually makes them, but you can never force him. Men who are forced are the ones who call the wedding off after you've ordered the cake and sent out the invitations. They are the ones who start running around the minute you get pregnant.

You don't *ever* want to force an unwilling man, but when you sense your man is willing, you can help make the next step easier for him.

Many men, after deciding that they want nothing more than to live with you, or to get married, will wait *forever* to ask. They are afraid of rejection, or are waiting for "the right moment," or are just plain bashful. How do you find out that he's already decided and is just waiting, for some reason, to ask?

You already know the techniques for getting him in the mood to agree with you. Now you will learn how to confirm that he actually is in the mood, before bringing up the delicate subject of long-term commitments. You will learn how to broach the subject in a way that will confirm his willingness. Once you know that, it's safe to proceed. He's probably hoping you will.

For example, you've become an exclusive couple, and you know he's very much in love with you. You would like to start living together, but you want to be sure he feels the same way before you ask him.

First, set the stage as you would for casting a spell. Use some loving memory anchors to get him in a receptive mood. Be sure you're totally in tune with him. Mirror him. Speak to him in his Love Language. Pick up on his rhythm. Breathe with him.

Then, shift your position into a new posture. If you've been sitting up straight, you could slump. Or you could lean forward or backward. *See if he follows your move.* If he doesn't, go back and start over mirroring him. Then try once more. If he still doesn't follow your lead, that tells you to let it go until another time.

If he is following your lead physically, start to lead him to the commitment you want—in progressive steps of agreement. At each step, shift position slightly. If he keeps following your physical lead, you know he's "in sync." It's a subtle but sure test that he's comfortable with the conversation, so you know you're safe to keep going.

You might shift from leaning forward to leaning back and say, "You know, it's getting very expensive to eat out if we want to see each other a lot."

He leans back and says, "Yeah, this is killing my budget. We can't go on like this."

He's not just agreeing, he's also following you physically. You know he's not feeling pressed, that he's actually very comfortable with where this is going.

You say, "It would be cheaper for us to eat at my place more often" (putting your arms on the back of your chair), "and we could even combine our grocery shopping."

He says (putting his arms on the back of his chair), "That's an interesting idea. I'd be willing to buy if you'd cook."

He's still following, so you know you're safe to pop the next question, the one you've been holding back. "Okay, let's start cooking at my place. We'll save lots of money, and you may even survive my cooking."

That's enough for now. End the conversation on a light note.

You have led him to agreement, slowly and safely. Planning on cooking and eating at home, at your place, is a significant little commitment. It's the first step toward living together. What's most important, you know it's really what he wanted. Final commitments follow from lesser commitments that work out well.

Now, if he hadn't leaned back while agreeing to the expense of eating out, you would have known to stop there—perhaps by just generally agreeing to be more budget conscious. Next, if he hadn't followed your lead by putting his arms on the back of the chair as you did, you would have known to stop with a sort of vague agreement to try a few meals at home.

On the other hand, if his response to your first suggestion about cutting expenses was, "I don't think it's eating out that's a problem, I think it's five-dollar movie tickets and two-dollar popcorn and four dollars for parking afterwards," you'd better take some time to rethink your whole approach. He *may* be ready to extend his commitment with you, but perhaps the next step should be to go in together on a cable television subscription.

Finally, if to your first suggestion about cutting expenses, he had said, "Oh, I don't mind buying us dinners out," it's clear he's not following in any sense. Stop immediately and consider whether you've misread him. Perhaps you don't know him as well as you thought you did. Review The Love Plan carefully. Be sure you're really talking his Love Language. Practice casting little spells to be sure you're "in sync."

Whatever you do, never try to push a man into a commitment of any kind before he's ready. Always test to confirm that he's really ready. There is no excuse for creating a deadly awkward moment or being put down. You should always know ahead of time when a man is ready to say yes.

Overcoming Resistance

Some men, after seemingly encouraging your hopes, will suddenly start resisting further commitment, or unexpectedly state that they're not ready to get any more involved. If you've been following The Love Plan, you know whether he loves you. You've also determined long befoιe this that he doesn't have some deep-down hangup about commitment. You know he loves you and is potentially capable of making a commitment. So what's wrong all of a sudden?

Something is bothering him. Now is not the time to get upset or to argue with him; now is the time to be supportive—and to find out gently what's bothering him. It's time for the artful use of the "How," "What," and "Why" questions, to unearth what his objections are. Only then can you deal with those objections.

For the visual lover, say something like, "It appears that you're concerned, and I want to look at the problem with you. What do you see that makes the future appear so cloudy for us?"

For the auditory lover, "It sounds like everything is not as harmonious with us as I thought, and I want to be totally in tune with you. Please tell me what you're thinking."

For the feelings lover, "I sense that something's troubling you about us. But you know your feelings are safe with me, so reach out and share them with me."

When Catherine came to me for advice, she was totally perplexed and frustrated. She and Gene had been living together for a year. Catherine was sure that Gene was basically very happy, and as much in love with her as she was with him. Yet he was obviously uncomfortable at any reference to commitments—even when discussing other couples.

Catherine found the right time and mood to tell Gene she sensed his discomfort, and she gently urged him to talk about it with her. Gene was, it turned out, equally frustrated. He wanted nothing more than to ask her to get married, but he felt he couldn't because a recent business failure had left him without enough money to support a wife.

Immensely relieved, Catherine was able to answer truthfully, "Oh, Gene. I don't love you for your money. This is a perfect time for us to get married.

If you had a lot of money, you'd be afraid of losing it in a divorce. This way you have nothing to lose. Our two salaries together will pay the bills. We're rich in love, and that's more valuable than money anyway."

By bringing a problem to light, and then contributing your own perspective to it, you may find that it isn't really a problem after all. Or he may change his mind about it after hearing your opinion. At the very least, once the problem is out in the open, you'll probably find it's not as bad as it was in your imagination. In Catherine and Gene's case, by the way, they were married not long after that conversation.

Advice from Friends

It's almost impossible to avoid getting relationship advice from friends. Everyone thinks he or she is an expert and knows what's best for you.

If your friends are wise enough not to volunteer advice, you're probably going to bring it on yourself. You naturally want to talk to your friends about the new love in your life. You want to ask advice, get pointers, or just hear them tell you how wonderful he is.

Unfortunately, the first time you tell a friend something that doesn't fit into his or her idea of the perfect "fantasy" relationship, you are likely to hear, "Oh, I wouldn't put up with that."

You have just told your best friend that you and your new love have the greatest sex life you've ever experienced. Every time you two are together you just can't wait to get home to bed. You and your lover are so happy you don't care about going out or watching television, all you want to do is make love.

Your best friend says haughtily, "Oh, I wouldn't put up with that."

"What do you mean?" you ask, really surprised.

"Well, I would want a man to take me out," she tells you righteously. "I mean what kind of relationship is that where all you do is go to bed together? Have you met his family? Doesn't he take you out to dinner? Aren't you afraid he'll find some other woman to go to movies with or take out to fancy restaurants?"

Suddenly, you're not as happy as you once were. Your new relationship doesn't look as good. The bloom is off the rose as you listen to your best friend tell you what she would and wouldn't put up with. Unfortunately, you don't know what she'd really put up with if she had a chance. Probably things you'd never imagine.

Don't Screw It Up

When you are in love, you will naturally have moments of doubt. Keep them to yourself. He probably has a few of his own. Hearing yours won't make him feel any better.

Don't be afraid to go for the gusto when it comes to love. You know the things that drive a man away —scenes and criticism.

You know the things that keep a man coming back—love, warmth, and emotional security. The choice is yours. Shower a man with real understanding, acceptance, and appreciation, and he'll come back time and time again. You know how to make him yours.

Keeping Love Alive

When you find the love you've been looking for, don't give up on The Love Plan. If you keep watching the signals your man is giving you, you will be able to read his mind forever. You will be able to keep him happy forever, but you must stay "in sync" with his inner self.

Start your discussions with agreements. Use The Love Plan techniques to resolve problems and avoid fights.

Keep practicing his Love Language until it becomes second nature to you. Pay attention to his words and his moods. Continue to mirror him, and never stop weaving your magic spells.

If you keep using The Love Plan, the man you love will always want to be with you. You alone will understand him completely. There isn't a man alive who can resist a woman with the knowledge and skill you have. You know the magic. You can create the "chemistry" of love. It will be with you alone that he finds love and security. He will be yours forever.